# LEATHERHEAD
## A History

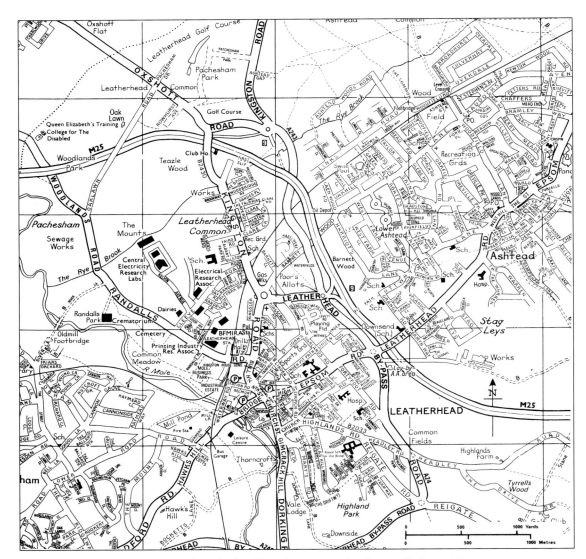

Modern map of Leatherhead based upon map by George Philip and Son.

# LEATHERHEAD
## A History

Edwina Vardey

Phillimore

2001

Published by
PHILLIMORE & CO. LTD.
Shopwyke Manor Barn, Chichester, West Sussex

ISBN 1 86077 189 0

Printed and bound in Great Britain by
BIDDLES LTD.
Guildford, Surrey

# Contents

# List of Illustrations

*Frontispiece*: Leatherhead town centre

# Acknowledgements

*Leatherhead: A History* is a revised, condensed and updated version of the *History of Leatherhead—a town at the crossroads*.

Once again I wish to acknowledge the help of those who worked with me on that book, published by the Leatherhead and District Local History Society in 1988 and 1989.

As well as a number of new illustrations, this book contains many used in the earlier book and for these I am very grateful to the History Society and for the assistance of its members.

My thanks to Goff Powell, Linda Heath, Gwen Hoad and Jeremy Early and especially to Peter Tarplee, the chairman of the Local History Society, who not only encouraged me in this project but actively and uncomplainingly gave me much technical support.

EDWINA VARDEY

Fetcham 2001

# Introduction

Leatherhead is somewhere between a town and a village. It is halfway along the River Mole and almost exactly in the centre of the old county of Surrey (before so much of it disappeared into Greater London). It is mid-way between Gatwick and Heathrow airports and is the mid-point of the railway line from Horsham to London.

The layout of Leatherhead has changed again and again. Few people arriving by rail notice the imposing station building of 1866 and even fewer travellers on the M25 realise that 2,000 years ago the fields alongside were ancient woodland; or that their motorway now crosses its Roman predecessor, built for fast traffic between Londinium, the capital, and Regnum (Chichester), the naval base. Even today's gypsy site on the Leatherhead bypass is close to where travellers first camped several thousand years ago.

Although called a county town, Leatherhead never rose above being a small town with a local market. It was concerned with the cloth trade during the Middle Ages. Later, its connection with agricultural estates saw it through economically until the beginning of the 20th century when cheap rail travel and an expansion of light engineering and research laboratories pointed local employment in new directions.

## The name of Leatherhead

Although leather-working and tanning were trades in the town as recently as 1905, Leatherhead does not get its name from leather. (In Victorian times the spelling was usually Letherhead, harking back to the medieval Latin version *Lered*.) The earliest known version is *Leodrindan*, an estate bequeathed by King Alfred about A.D. 880. It has usually been translated as the 'public ford' from the Old English words *leode* and *ride*, but an alternative has recently been put forward: grey (or brown—*llwyd*) ford from the Celtic *letorito*. The River Mole at Leatherhead was fordable in many places, although today crossings are usually by a bridge.

## The landscape of Leatherhead

The parish of Leatherhead lies mainly on the east or right bank of the River Mole after it emerges through the North Downs at Mickleham. The northern half of Leatherhead lies on London Clay. Further south is the Upper Chalk with a narrow band of well-drained clays and gravels between the two. Geologically these strata are quite young.

The River Mole created the Mickleham Gap, and the Leatherhead-Dorking road still follows the flood plain through it. Climate changes resulted in several gravel terraces being laid down beside the river, and fissures in the chalk were dissolved to produce the 'swallow holes', a feature of the river bed in times of drought when the water flows down these fissures as though down the plug hole of an enormous bath tub.

Except at flood-time, the Mole is a very sluggish stream through Leatherhead, varying

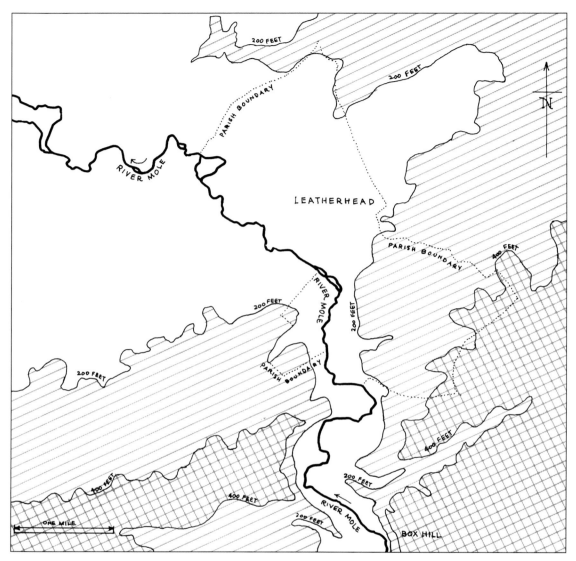

**1**  Contour map showing the River Mole winding through the gap in the North Downs.

considerably in width. Some man-made alterations to its course can be seen: the ornamental
canal at Thorncroft, the railway embankment
crossing a meander at Cannon Court, Fetcham,
and straightening at the site of the former bridge
at Young Street.

The old name for the river was Emele
and later Emlyn; Mole only appears in the 16th
century. The name's being due to the 'swallow

hole' phenomenon has been challenged and
suggested alternative theories are of a back-
formation from Molesey (Mul's Island) or from
the Latin for mill (mol).

The ice sheet covering what is now
southern England retreated northward about
10,000 years ago, leaving behind a wetter but
warmer climate than that of today. As vegeta-
tion returned, alder bushes predominated on

the marshy ground. Birch and hazel dominated the lighter soils, with beech and lime on the chalk downland and oak with hornbeam on the lower claylands. Yew and box groves cling to the sides of Box Hill and give some idea of what the early landscape of Leatherhead may have been, and with so many varied habitats in the area it is not surprising that 500 species of wild plants, including shrubs and trees, have been recorded.

## Wildlife

Most rare animals in the area are nocturnal; even so, the roe deer can often be seen in woodland in early evening. Where Stane Street crosses the M25, the motorway contractors built a tunnel for badgers in a small attempt to stem the decline in their population. There are no such worries about the fox who wanders fearlessly both day and night, often making its lair in gardens. There are hopes that the otter may eventually return to the Mole. Among the smaller mammals, the dormouse is now an endangered species. Rare butterflies and moths seen on Box Hill and Fetcham Downs include the marbled white, dark green fritillary, common blue, silver-spotted skipper and purple and green hairstreak.

In winter, visiting migrant birds such as redpoll and siskin can be found in the riverside alders while waders like the common sandpiper appear in spring and autumn. The heron can be seen throughout the year. Breeding birds like mute swan, mallard, little grebe, kingfisher and grey wagtail have recently been joined by the mandarin duck. There is an established population of feral birds like the ring-necked parakeet who seem to be able to survive the winters. Birds of prey like sparrowhawks and kestrels are recovering from 19th-century persecution and 20th-century pesticides while hobbies have bred locally in recent years. Nightingales are much less numerous but can still be heard on Bookham Common.

**2** View from Hawks Hill, *c.*1850.

*Chapter One*

# Prehistory to the Middle Ages
## *c.*4000 B.C.–A.D. 600

The earliest traces of human occupation at Leatherhead so far discovered are flints dating from the Mesolithic period around 4000 B.C. The people of that time were fishermen and hunters, eating fruit, plants and nuts. They may have cleared some open forest but as they were not farmers they tended to move on. Three Mesolithic hearths of burnt birch-wood, covered in worked flints, were found about five feet down when a new channel for the river was cut at Young Street in 1952. A se-

lection of flints, mainly cores and scrapers, the residue of a factory perhaps, is shown below. The fine complete tranchet axe came from rather deeper down than the rest, and was found some way away from them. The quality of the workmanship was not exceptionally high.

About 3000 B.C. the climate became colder and drier, and the forest covering became thinner. By 2000 B.C. most of the upland had been cleared of forest. Stone tools of this Neolithic period range from the crude flint axe

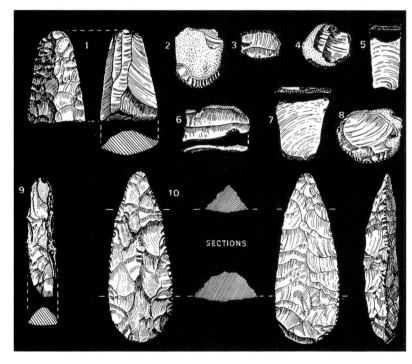

**3** Some of the many flints found in 1952 when a new river channel was cut at Young Street. The most valuable is no. 10, a tranchet axe, probably a digging tool.

1

4   Celtic bronze roundel found on a clay hill opposite Dorincourt.

found in a Highlands Avenue garden to a fragment of a fine polished one dredged from the river near Young Street, and the macehead made of quartzite pebble whose battered end and worn hole for the wooden handle point to use for hammering.

About 1800 B.C. a new wave of immigrants, able to work metals and in particular bronze, arrived. Bronze was scarce and a trading system had to be set up to maintain supplies of ore and to sell the products. A trackway, known as the Harroway, came into use. It extended from Kent as far as Hampshire and Wiltshire. In Surrey, it roughly followed the line of the present-day towns and villages between Croydon and Farnham. It probably entered Leatherhead from the east along Green Lane, turning south-west along the Epsom Road to cross the river about where the Leisure Centre is now and climb Hawks Hill through the waterworks land.

Aerial views show many burial mounds (barrows or tumuli) near Thirty Acres Barn. One barrow near Cherkley Court was excavated and burial urns were found. All these barrows probably date from the Bronze or Iron Age.

The only true Bronze-Age finds come from the floodplain near Young Street: some flint arrowheads and a disc-knife; scratches in the flint contain iron pyrites, probably from the Wealden ironstone pebble used to smooth it.

About 500 B.C. the climate became warmer and wetter and beech trees spread on the chalk, as did oak and alder on the clay. Celtic tribes, displaced by the Roman invasions of France, moved into Britain bringing with them the ability to till heavy soils with an improved plough which had a mould-board to turn over the earth. Constant ploughing in one direction caused the soil to creep downhill to the edge of the field, and the consequent banks (lynchets) can be traced on the ground or from the air. There are many such banks and enclosures surrounding the Iron-Age farm at the top of Hawks Hill, Fetcham and traces of fields on Leatherhead and Mickleham Downs. Several 'Celtic' fields flank a double-ditched trackway just north-east of Cherkley Court and a large oval enclosure nearby may be the site of the settlement itself. Belgic coins have been found in two Leatherhead gardens. One is a copy of a stater of Philip of Macedon, current in Gaul after the plunder of Greece in 278 B.C. Iron-Age pottery has been found at Woodlands Park and Givons Grove.

At Woodlands Park, the occupation of the hilltop seems to have gone on throughout the Roman period, but exactly what form the activities took is not clear. A flint-paved and drained area produced pottery fragments dating from as late as the 4th century A.D., together with an enamelled roundel with a trumpet-like pattern. Scattered Roman pottery and coins have turned up elsewhere, particularly when the Tyrrells Wood golf course was being laid out.

## Roman Leatherhead
The Roman development of Leatherhead was agricultural, using the woodlands for building and fuel. Excavation of the Romano-British farmsteads at the top of Hawks Hill, Fetcham

revealed burnt grains, storage pits and drying ovens as well as the post-holes of the farm buildings themselves. On the other side of Leatherhead, the heavy clays north of Ashtead were used in a large brickworks, whose products were often re-used elsewhere. There are Roman bricks in Leatherhead and Fetcham parish churches and a quantity of Roman glass, tiles and pottery were found on the site of the medieval manor house of Pachenesham.

Part of the parish boundary, Stane Street is the Roman road running in a straight line from London to Chichester, with 'service areas' at Ewell and Dorking. From Dorking to Burford

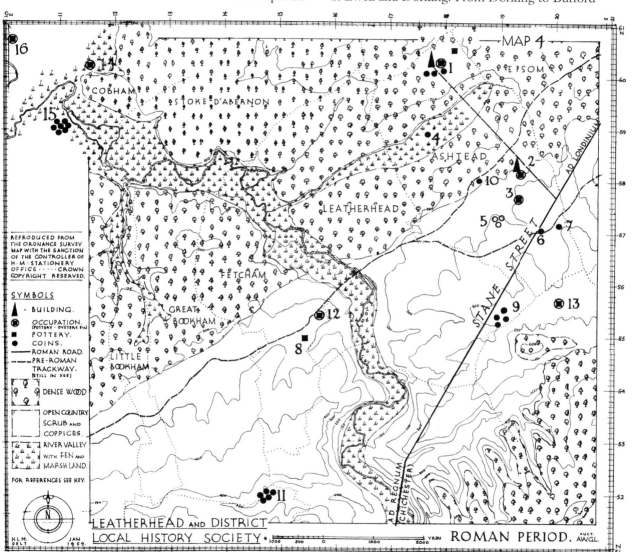

5   Roman Leatherhead map showing finds (1) an A.D. 200 brickworks and villa; (2) building near Ashtead church; (3) corn pits and pottery found in Ashtead; (4 and 5) coins found in Ashtead; (6 and 7) lynch pin found in Stane Street and coin; (8) pottery at Young Street; (9) coins on Tyrrells Wood golf course; (10) bronze key ring at Ashtead; (11) hoard of coins at Blagdon Farm Bookham; (12) corn pits ovens, pottery and brooches at Hawks Hill; (13) sites at Headley and Cobham.

the exact line of the road is uncertain, but beyond Juniper Hill it can be followed as a footpath (Pebble Lane) north-eastward over Mickleham Downs and beyond to Epsom. Aerial photographs indicate that it was about 55ft. wide, including side ditches, although the one section cut across Stane Street showed only a 15ft. width of metalling with flints set in sand in the manner of the 18th-century turn-pikes.

**The Anglo-Saxon settlement**

After the withdrawal of the Roman army and administration in A.D. 410, the Saxon settlement began in the southern coastal regions. By the late 6th century there were pagan Saxon cemeteries in north-east Surrey. Place-names suggest that the colonisation of central Surrey took place by way of the Weald, the pioneers pushing up the side valley from the rivers. Over the last 200 years a very extensive Saxon

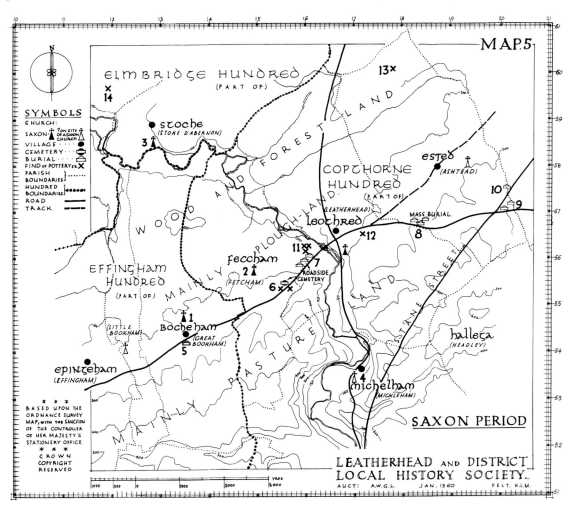

6   Saxon period map. (1, 2, 3, 4 and 5) Bookham, Fetcham, Leatherhead, Stoke d'Abernon and Mickleham churches; (6) skeletons found in 1953 in Bookham Grove; (7) Saxon cemetery, Hawks Hill; (8) mass burial found in 1927 beside Green Lane; (9) burials south of Ashtead Park found in 1910; (10) burial in Stane Street, 1932; (11) objects found in Watersmeet, Fetcham in 1929 and 1930; (12) Saxon pin and pottery found in the garden of Leatherhead Hospital; and (13) Saxon spearhead found in 1926 at Cobham.

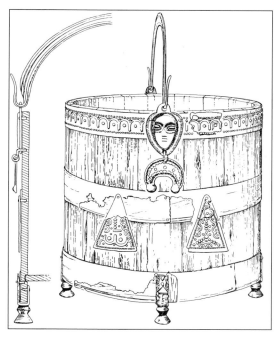 

**7** A wooden bucket with bronze attachments found at Fetcham millpond in 1929. Reconstructed here in a drawing by David Williams and reproduced with permission of SAC.

**8** In 1985 over thirty skeletons were unearthed in Ermyn Way when the Goblin Works was demolished and Esso was building a new headquarters on the site. It was a Saxon pagan cemetery.

**9** Rob Poulton of SAC is examining one of the skeletons, buried in a foetal position with hands placed as if to grasp a staff, and an iron spearhead found nearby.

cemetery has been discovered piecemeal on both sides (and under) the modern road running up Hawks Hill, just over the Fetcham boundary. A mass grave-pit, cut 6-8 feet deep in the chalk alongside Green Lane in Ermyn Way, was found in 1927 and a Saxon spearhead was found nearby 50 years later. A faceted pin and potsherds dated A.D. 800 came from a garden near the hospital which was once part of the Common Field. Swords, spearheads and parts of a decorated bucket were found on the site of the present fire station.

In 1985 the Goblin Works in Ermyn Way was demolished and several graves were uncovered. Esso, who owned the site, generously funded a full excavation. Nearly thirty skeletons of men, women and children were found. Seventeen graves were all aligned with the heads to the west. In some, the bodies were laid on their backs; in others, they were crouched on their sides. Most graves carried artifacts. Two of the men were buried with their spears and most had iron knives. One spearhead was exceptionally long. The graves of the women contained a bone comb, beads and a panther shell, probably a fertility symbol, and a necklace of shells similar to those from the Red Sea. One male had been decapitated and the head was buried between his ankles. The artifacts showed that these were pagans of around the sixth or seventh century.

The other skeletons, all male, were in ill-formed rough holes, not as defined as the other graves, and with no artifacts. Several of them had been beheaded and the position of the bones of the hands, some in front and some behind, indicated they had been tied together and probably executed. Late 12th-century pottery was found in a large hole suggesting a gibbet had been erected there. Judging by the close proximity to the regular graves, these were criminals buried at a later time by Christians in a place known by them to have been a pagan cemetery.

## Chapter Two

# The Early Middle Ages *c*.600–1250

By the 13th century Leatherhead had assumed the form of a roughly hourglass-shaped parish with the town at its centre. South-eastwards, on fertile land following the dip-slope of the Downs, lay the intensively farmed Common Field. West of this, crossing the river and sweeping up towards Fetcham, was a block of old enclosures, and around the southern edge of the cultivated land lay the high open Downs. The north half of the parish consisted entirely of enclosed fields, ascending to the heavy, wooded London Clay. The town is one of a series of settlements strung out along an old west-east trackway which follows the dip-slope. Geography explains the strip-like form of parishes in this area: each was an economic

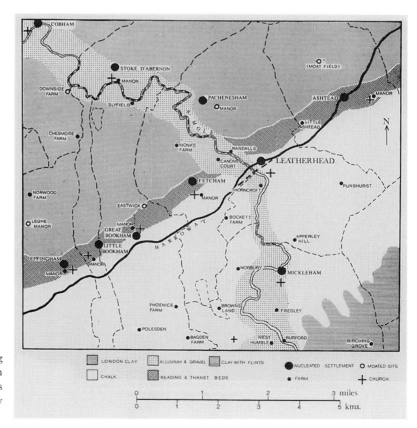

**10** Geological map showing medieval settlement and parish boundaries. All the farm sites were probably in existence by *c*.1300.

unit, its main settlement lying near good arable land between downland pasture for sheep and woodland pasture for cattle.

Once it was assumed that this pattern of settlement and economy was stamped on the landscape by the earliest Anglo-Saxons. But now it is known that villages and common fields are the end-product of a long evolution, the crucial stages of which probably lie in the 10th and 11th centuries. To rediscover Anglo-Saxon Leatherhead the picture of the integrated village and parish community must be set aside, and a search made among the farms and field-boundaries for traces of a lost older world. In that world, Leatherhead was of more than local importance not as a town but as a key place in the systematic 'local government' of mid-Saxon England: a centre of royal authority and the site of a minster church.

## The royal vill

Great advances have been made lately in understanding how kings exercised power within the early kingdoms. It seems that Hundreds, the basic units of local government from the 10th century onwards, are merely subdivisions of larger, earlier territories which had taken shape at least by the late 7th century. At the heart of each territory lay a king's manor-house or royal vill (*regia villa* in Latin, *cyninges tun* in English) from which law was administered on the king's behalf. The governmental centre was also the economic centre: the territory was assessed according to a regular structured system of taxes which its inhabitants owed to the royal vill.

Reconstructing the early boundaries must be speculative, but there are grounds for thinking that Copthorne, Effingham and Wotton Hundreds may represent an early territory running in a broad strip from the London Clay, across the Downs and through the Weald to the Sussex border. Copthorne and Effingham Hundreds shared one meeting-place, and a large tract of downland which crossed the two Hundreds but was known by the single name of 'Polesden' suggests an early

unity. One aspect of the early economy—the seasonal driving of pigs from the more open lands to fatten in the Wealden woods has left clues in the form of Wealden land attached to manors several miles northwards, such as Newdigate parish, on the Sussex border, much of which belonged to manors in Leatherhead, Ashtead and Ewell. Two peasant holdings there can be traced in the records of Thorncroft manor, Leatherhead, from the 1270s onwards, recalling the days when every year Leatherhead pigs were driven 10 miles to root among the acorns of Newdigate.

Leatherhead was a royal vill, one of five in Surrey listed in King Alfred's will (879-888). In Domesday Book (1086, with data for 1066) such ancient centres often still appear as royal manors, and in Surrey some are immediately obvious: Godalming, Woking, Wallington, Stoke-by-Guildford and, of course, Kingston. By 1066 the two manors of Leatherhead were both in private hands, but there are good grounds for identifying the lost royal centre with Pachenesham in the north-west of the parish. It has the oldest place-name in the parish, 'Paeccin's *ham*' (homestead), and was probably established in the first stages of English settlement. In the 13th century this manor was held for services associated with royal justice: finding a prison, a pound for beasts distrained for the king's debt, and a bench for the county court where it was normally held. This is supported by a statement of the county jurors in 1259 that the county court, recently moved to Guildford, had 'always' been held at Leatherhead. It seems that Leatherhead was remembered as a place which had once had important judicial functions, and that these were linked in some way to Pachenesham.

## The minster

Leatherhead also had an ancient and important church, one of those churches known by the 10th century as the 'old minsters'. Mostly founded in the early days of English Christianity, they were collegiate churches supporting 'team

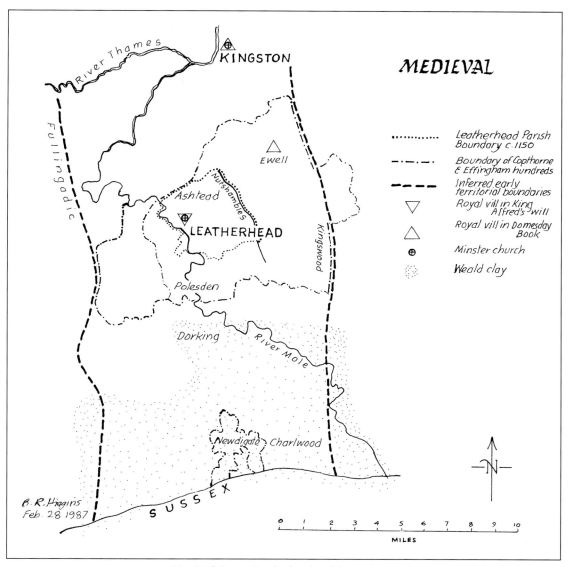

**11**  Mid-Saxon Leatherhead and its territory.

ministries', groups of priests who served large territories equivalent in size to several later parishes. Between royal vill and minster there was often a close link. Many minsters were founded by kings at their vills; the minster parish might be identical with the vill's territory, and church finance might be based directly on existing secular taxation. But as thousands of local churches were founded in the 10th and 11th centuries, the minsters lost most of their pastoral role and much of their wealth and status. In Domesday Book their endowments are often annexed to support royal clerks or other absentees.

What happened to the old minster? The answer to this question is not the obvious one—

that it became the parish church—since this seems to have been founded separately to serve the Domesday manor of Thorncroft. But an enclave of land in the north of the parish, near the medieval centre of Pachenesham (and so probably near the lost royal vill), is first recorded in the 13th century as held of Ewell manor for 20s. rent. This suggests an intriguing possibility that the minster church simply disappeared, its Domesday valuation of 20s. remaining fossilised as a rent from the former glebeland, and somewhere in the Pachenesham area an Anglo-Saxon church may still await the archaeologist. The minster's parochial rights must have been transferred to the estate church of Thorncroft, more conveniently sited near the river-crossing, which thus emerges with jurisdiction over Leatherhead parish and Ashtead chapelry. It can be shown, for instance, that almost exactly the same thing happened at Godalming, again leaving a deserted minster site. Both cases illustrate what seems to be a general pattern: major changes in settlement between the 10th and 13th centuries which left ancient centres redundant.

## Early land-units and boundaries

One of the strongest forces for change in late Anglo-Saxon England was the swift advance of the break-up of great complex territories, each containing numerous settlements but run from one royal or monastic centre, to provide thousands of smaller, private lordships. What are now thought of as 'normal' or 'parish-sized' manors have been proliferating in the 10th and 11th centuries, and with them came manor-houses and manorial churches. Also established well before the Conquest was the distinction between 'demesne' (farmed directly by the lord) and smallholdings (in the hands of tenants) which was to be basic to all manorial history. Great changes in rural settlement and economy were linked to the needs of a relatively new class of minor gentry.

The territory once ruled from Leatherhead royal vill had fragmented by 1066 into a series of strip-like manors divided across Effingham,

Great and Little Bookham, Fetcham and Ashtead. Between the last two lay what is now known as Leatherhead, but in Domesday Book it is not described as such. Instead there are entries for two manors, Pachenesham and Thorncroft, which between them comprised the later parish area. Perhaps the name 'Leatherhead' (*Leodridan* in Alfred's will, *Leret* in Domesday Book) had once denoted the whole territory of the royal vill.

In Edward the Confessor's time, 'Aelmer' (Aethelmaer or Aelfmaer) held the main part of Pachenesham (four hides), apparently from royal demesne; Earl Harold held another 1¼ hides, with Leofric and 'Aelmer' (presumably the same man) holding under him. Thorncroft was in the hands of Cola, a Surrey thegn who also held Betchworth and Coombe; with some extra lands (1¼ hides held by Merwin, one hide held by Aelfric and 'Aelmer' and one hide held by Coleman the hunter) it supported the very large assessment of 25½ hides.

The demesne lands of Pachenesham were essentially the north-west part of the parish, while those of Thorncroft lay in the south-west though with some fields on the east parish boundary towards Ashtead. At first sight the Common Field seems to prove an economic unity between the two manors, as their tenants' strips lay intermixed. But close analysis suggests that in the late Middle Ages only about ten per cent of these strips were held of Pachenesham, the remainder belonging to Thorncroft or its offshoots. It looks very much as though the Common Field is of Thorncroft origin, and that the two manors had once lain as separate blocks: Thorncroft was the south half of the parish plus some land along its north-east boundary, and Pachenesham was the remainder.

How, then, did 'Leatherhead' come into being? It may be partly parochial, partly topographical. Following a common pattern, it is the 'rump' of the old minster parish left by the carving-out of local parishes. Fetcham, Mickleham and the Bookhams had independent churches before records started, while Ashtead church, originally a chapel of Leatherhead, was free by *c.*1200; Thorncroft and Pachenesham were simply what remained. At the same time, the growth of a small town on the boundary between the two manors created a physical and commercial focus. Developments in agriculture, and in the land-market, gradually brought about an intermixture of holdings and a sharing of resources which forged Pachenesham and Thorncroft into one economic unit. It is symptomatic that Thorncroft church assumed the attributes of the abandoned minster and a new status as Leatherhead church. So medieval Leatherhead is best visualised as two fragments of the old royal territory, split tenurially but re-combined around a new centre.

Manor and parish boundaries often preserve landmarks from a pre-manorial age. One such is the linear bank called 'Nutshambles' which divides Ashtead and Headley on the west from Epsom and Walton on the east. The name appears in 1496 as *Motschameles* and seems likely to mean *mot scaemol*, 'the seat of the moot'. The convergence of many roads at a high point on the line of the earthwork suggests an important meeting-place, possibly a primitive folk-moot in the territory of Leatherhead vill.

Another case is more intriguing. The block of Thorncroft demesne fields along the north-east boundary of the parish is almost rectilinear, defined as two rough squares. Eastwards lay the manor of Little Ashtead and Ashtead common field bounded by the intersecting alignments of Barnett Wood Lane, Ottways Lane, Woodfield Lane, Skinners Lane and Harriots Lane to form two more rough squares of almost identical size. Viewed as a whole, the area looks as though it has been deliberately laid out on an irregular grid-plan—and one which is respected by manor and parish boundaries. Close at hand lies the Ashtead Roman villa and tile works, with a possible road link to Stane Street on the alignment of the grid. All this suggests the remarkable conclusion that boundaries connected with the villa survived to define land-units throughout the Anglo-Saxon period.

## Manors and landlords after the Conquest

Pachenesham, like many manors, was held in 1086 by the king's rapacious half-brother, Odo of Bayeux. Two tenants, Ranulf and Baynard, had the portions held under Earl Harold in Edward the Confessor's day. When Odo fell two years later, it reverted to royal demesne, which may have been its status until shortly before the Conquest. Pachenesham should probably be identified with the 100s. rent in Leatherhead which Hugh de St Omer held of the Crown from before 1155 until 1161. In 1198 Richard I granted 10s. rent there to William de Eys, whose descendants held it until 1233 when it passed to Matthew Bezille. King John granted the larger portion of Pachenesham to Brian de Therfeld ('the usher') in 1203, when it was valued at 70s. 2d., to be held at the yearly rent of a Norwegian falcon. It descended to Brian's son-in-law, Philip de Thorp of Essex; his heir Walter was overlord in *c.*1300, when it was still being called 'the King's fee'.

In 1086 Thorncroft was a demesne manor of another great Norman lord, Richard fitz Gilbert, founder of the honour of Clare. The church is not mentioned in Domesday Book, but it probably existed by the 1080s and passed as a dowry to Richard's son-in-law Eudes the Sewer. A generation later, the rest of the manor formed the dowry of Richard's grand-daughter, Margaret, on her marriage to an Essex knight named William de Montfichet. In *c.*1190 Richard de Montfichet, grandson of William and Margaret, sold Thorncroft to John de Cherbrugh, a Wiltshire knight who lived to a great age and held the manor until *c.*1260.

The Eys, Therfeld, Thorp and Montfichet families were all non-resident, drawing revenues from Leatherhead but having little to do with local concerns. John de Cherburgh was more active in Copthorne Hundred affairs and maintained a household at Thorncroft, but it was still only one of his manors. In the 12th century, however, a gentry family was established who long remained the principal local residents and who took the surname 'de Leatherhead'. By *c.*1300 they lived on a small manor in the north of Leatherhead parish known as 'Little Pachenesham', later Randalls, where a mansion has always existed until replaced by the Randalls Park Crematorium. The origins of this property are obscure. It seems to have been held under the d'Abernons, tenants of Clare and Warenne in nearby Fetcham and Stoke, so it may derive from a manor on the Fetcham bank of the river rather than from Domesday Pachenesham.

The key to this family's origins is a charter, issued by Margaret de Montfichet in *c.*1170, establishing title to land in the south of the parish which they held of Thorncroft manor. Margaret recounts how her husband William, on his deathbed, had asked her to restore to the heirs of Fulk son of Amfrid of Thorncroft, slain in his service, the land which Fulk had

held. Accordingly, she confirms to Amfrid son of Fulk his father's lands, comprising half a hide in Thorncroft and a mill, and further grants him 'the hide which Ailwin and Hugh de Punesherst and Fulk de Punesherst and Ailmer hold', and a virgate in Aperderle which he already holds in demesne.

By remarkable good luck, a correlation of the rents specified in this charter with a rental of *c.*1300 makes possible an almost complete identification of the lands. What Margaret confirmed and granted to Amfrid was the farm and fields south-west of Thorncroft later called Bockett Farm (probably the original half-hide); a holding (probably the de Punesherts' hide) of about 127 acres, a quarter in a field called Joyesfield on the Headley boundary and the rest dispersed in the Common Field; and fields along the east bank of the Mole to the south of Thorncroft manor (the virgate in 'Aperderle'). In doing this, she cut a big slice out of the Thorncroft demesne lands as well as alienating lordship over several common field holdings.

The endowment of knights with portions of demesne land was common in Anglo-Norman England and Fulk son of Amfrid's original half-hide was evidently in this category. Much larger than the average peasant farm, it was small by the standard of Domesday military holdings and represented only a fraction of the knight's fee for which the whole manor of Thorncroft was held. The family presumably originated as soldiers in the Montfichet entourage; the names Amfrid and Fulk are both Norman rather than English. Fulk was slain in William de Montfichet's service, and since William himself was dead by the early 1150s, it seems likely that this happened during the civil war of Stephen's reign. We see here the modest holding of a man-at-arms who held his land for actual military service. By contrast, after *c.*1170 Fulk's son Amfrid was to hold the land by hereditary succession and at sizeable rents; he was more a resident proprietor than an armed retainer. The family appear regularly

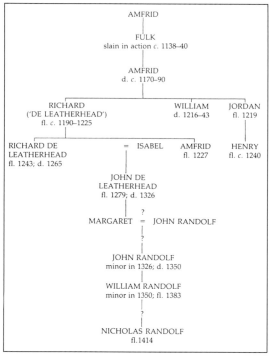

**12**   The descendants of Norman man-at-arms Amfrid took the name 'de Ledrede' (Leatherhead) and later generations became minor gentry. It is possible their descendants' name 'Randolf' may have led to a corruption and their land became 'Randalls'.

thereafter, and were calling themselves 'de Ledrede' (Leatherhead) by the 1220s. By *c.*1300 John de Leatherhead was holding the Montfichet land jointly with 'Little Pachenesham', and on his death in 1326 the inheritance passed to his daughter's son John. This man was probably John Randolf, head of a family which held the joint manor for at least three generations and from whom it was to be called 'Randalls'. Thus the descendants of a man-at-arms maintained on one of his lord's demesnes were transformed into minor gentry by the later Middle Ages.

## The farming community

In Midland England the pressures of an intensive grain-producing economy necessitated, at least by the 12th century, communal and highly organised farming systems. Surrey, by contrast, belongs to the 'wood-pasture' zone, in which an abundance of wastes and commons allowed the agricultural community to remain relatively free and unstructured. Leatherhead is no exception; there were still large commons on the clay northwards and the Downs southwards, and less than half the arable lay in scattered intermixed strips in the Common Field. So it comes as no surprise to find a community of prosperous farmers, most of whom held by free tenure.

While the de Leatherheads were the main local family, several others appear when records become fuller after 1200 and are mentioned regularly in deeds and lawsuits. Foremost among these were the de Aperdeles, the de Punshursts (already mentioned in Margaret de Montfichet's charter), the de Bradmeres, the del Broks, the de Oxencrofts, the le Hores and the Pinchuns. These people cannot be called peasants; they were substantial freeholders, frequently occupied in the affairs of Copthorne Hundred and in private litigation. Such independent, well-established farming families are characteristic of 12th- and 13th-century Surrey, making it more like the free society of Kent than the servile peasant communities of the Midlands.

Lesser families are rarely mentioned. Usually the humble only appear in Assize Rolls which record their crimes or violent deaths. Thus it is known that Bernard the miller of Pachenesham was crushed to death by a cart in 1235, and that Levina daughter of William Baynguard was raped at Leatherhead by William Balemund in 1241; while a roll for 1224-5 lists the delightful names of two Leatherhead sheep-stealers, William Bullfinch and Henry Chop.

It may be an important distinction between the greater and lesser families that the former usually lived in farmsteads which stood apart on the enclosed fields of their farms. Thirteenth-century Leatherhead, like the adjoining parishes, had a pattern of dispersed settlement which was probably older than the villages. The manor houses of Pachenesham, 'Little Pachenesham' and Thorncroft all stood alone. The main families took their names from locations within the parish (Aperdele, Punshurst, Bradmere and Oxencroft appear later as field names on the Gwilt map) and there they must have lived. The old Aperdele homestead can be traced through the Thorncroft records from *c.*1275 to a map of 1629, where it is shown as a deserted enclosure called Apperley Hill.

## The Common Field

In the Common Field matters were very different. Originally there may have been compact farms here too, some memory of which is preserved in furlong and landmark names suggesting ancient proprietorship: Buntanlond, Dondene, Edolvesdone, Godhivedene, Katebardene, Kenchescrofte, Lomleshegg, Lyndene, Swyndolvestorne, Tibeliesdene, Tonnerscroft. Partible inheritance and a growing demand for land on the fertile strip during the late Anglo-Saxon period would have caused progressive fragmentation of holdings into scattered strips. Manorial records show that by 1270 these strips were apportioned between tenants in regular 13-acre shares. Rentals of both Thorncroft and Little Pachenesham show this feature; since the Common Field holdings of these manors were separated in *c.*1170, the apportionment must have occurred at some earlier date. There is probably a glimpse here of a deliberate act of planning, by some late Anglo-Saxon or Norman lord of Thorncroft, which involved reorganising the Common Field into uniform subdivided holdings, probably with uniform rents and services to match.

The Common Field is a smaller and simpler version of a 'classic' Midland system, organised, integrated and regular. The tenants may have lived side by side in some nucleated 'Thorncroft village' (on and around Church Road is a likely area) which was later obscured by the growth of the town. This little community first evolved, and was then planned and organised within the old haphazard landscape of dispersed farms. But it never obliterated it completely, for Leatherhead shares the distinctive Surrey character of combining the 'primitive' mid-Saxon with the 'developed' Saxo-Norman pattern of organisation.

## The origins of the town

As suggested, the town must lie near the early boundary between Thorncroft and Pacheneshan. The church, Thorncroft's in origin, is not far away, and near it may have been a Thorncroft peasant settlement. On the other hand, Pachenesham had a bigger Domesday population than Thorncroft. Later evidence seems to show the bulk of town centre tenements attached to Pachenesham, while the market rights belonged to its lord. By the late 11th century, tenants from Pachenesham may already have established a permanent settlement near the river-crossing.

An important piece of topographical evidence is the town street pattern, which seems to be based on an earlier layout. Elm Road, now merely a small lane behind the High Street, can be projected westwards along a straight tenement boundary and the parish boundary to join the main road on Hawks Hill, continuing the course of the old trackway with less deviation than the line of Bridge Street and High

Street. Near the Thorndike Theatre car park, Elm Road turns a right-angle into Church Walk, which joins Worple Road to form a trackway running south towards Dorking. Worple Road divided the Common Field eastwards from the main Thorncroft demesne westwards, and Common Field strips were aligned on it.

Almost certainly, at the junction of Elm Road and Church Walk there was an early crossing of the main west-east route by a north-south trackway. Thorncroft manor lay south of the main road, with the trackway dividing its enclosed demesne from its open field. Subsequently a different alignment was superimposed on this crossroads, obliterating its northern and western arms. It is at least a reasonable hypothesis that some lord of Pachenesham required a street pattern from which tenement plots could be laid out on all sides over his own territory, without impinging on Thorncroft land.

Throughout England, the 12th and early 13th centuries saw urban growth and rapid expansion of internal trade. Landowners were quick to see the advantages of founding and fostering market towns on their manors, from which they could expect returns in rent and market tolls. Thus many small towns appear in these years; others, based on existing market centres, were enlarged or replanned. In Surrey there are the examples of Farnham, Haslemere, Reigate and Bletchingley, the last an especially relevant parallel in that it seems to have been replanned around an existing boundary crossroads shortly before appearing as a town in the 1220s. It seems very likely that Leatherhead as we now know it appeared in similar circumstances and at a similar date. A royal grant in 1248 of a weekly market and annual fair at Leatherhead (confirmed to the lord of Pachenesham Magna in 1331) may have been connected with its foundation. However founded, the town and its market were henceforth to provide a focus for Leatherhead and to dominate the lives of its people.

## Chapter Three

# The Late Middle Ages 1250–1558

In 13th-century England the population rose, markets grew and the economy flourished. Inflation from 1180 to 1220 began more than a century of high prices, happy years for all who could send surplus crops to market.

    Great landlords, previously content to draw fixed rents from their demesne estates, now took them under direct control. This was the age of 'high farming' in which the wealthy and powerful concerned themselves with agriculture and estate management, and spent lavishly on manor houses, barns and equipment.

### The manors and their lands 1250–1350

The account rolls, court rolls and private deeds show a world in which life was becoming more varied and material prosperity was growing for all but the poorest classes. They also provide

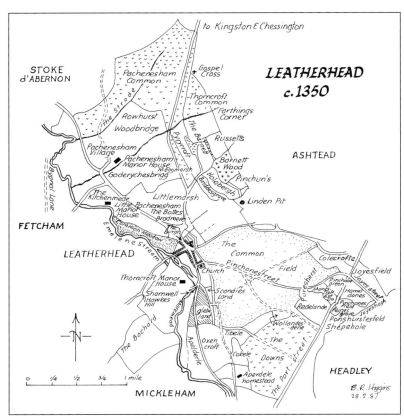

**13**   The intersection of roads from Kingston to Dorking and from Epsom to Guildford was already established in the Middle Ages.

15

the field names and topographical data from which the first detailed view of the Leatherhead landscape can be reconstructed.

By 1250 Leatherhead was a united community to the extent that it had one main settlement and one common field, but manorially it remained divided. Pachenesham was still in some sense distinct from Thorncroft or Leatherhead; thus a petition of *c*.1330 is in the name of 'the poor people of Leatherhead and of Pachenesham', and refers to 'the same vills'.

## Pachenesham

Between 1286 and 1343 Pachenesham, the old royal manor, had lords who were civil servants, their lives based more on the court than on Leatherhead. In 1286 the manor passed to Sir Eustace de Hacche, a busy administrator whose duties included building works at Edward I's castles. Little of his time can have been spent at Pachenesham, but he did maintain a household there where his grandson was born in 1291. Hacche died in 1306; two years later Edward II granted the manor to his favourite, Gaveston, who sold it in 1309 to Robert Darcy. Darcy, like Hacche before him, was in the king's service but lived intermittently at Leatherhead.

His attitude to his tenants and neighbours there seems to have been rapacious and aggressive, especially during the three years after Edward II's murder in 1327 when he was favoured by the Mortimer government. He consistently refused the old 20s. rent to Ewell manor, and made use of his influence at court when the lord of Ewell (by then Merton Priory) finally distrained on his cattle in 1327. In 1328 Darcy was himself distrained on the vicar of Leatherhead for failing to find a chaplain to serve St Margaret's chapel in Pachenesham Manor. In 1330 the local inhabitants complained of oppressions which he and his bailiffs had inflicted on them since obtaining judicial rights through Mortimer, and Sir John d'Abernon protested that Darcy had demolished his pillory at Leatherhead.

Hacche and Darcy had enough interest in Pachenesham to improve the manor house. Today a deserted, tree-grown moat, it was excavated by the Leatherhead and District Local History Society between 1946 and 1953. The site seems to have been occupied well before 1200, but in the 13th century the moat was dug and provided with a cluster of buildings dominated by a large hall. Unfortunately, dating of the excavated buildings remains imprecise,

**14** Reconstruction by A.G.W. Lowther of Pachesnesham manor house, 'The Mounts', at the time of Sir Eustace Hacche.

but it is presumed that some were the work of Hacche or Darcy, and perhaps of both. In 1293 Hacche was accused of having taken horses and carts from strangers at Kingston market to carry timber to his manor of Pachenesham, and this may well have been for building the hall.

The Pachenesham demesne surrounded the manor house in the north-west of the parish. Northwards they extended to the Stoke d'Abernon, Fetcham and Chessington boundaries, southwards to the damp soil north of the town called Meggmarsh and Littlemarsh. This was heavy unsympathetic land, its northern half covered with the woodland and scrub, so it seems unlikely that there was much cultivation north of the Rye Brook in the early 13th century.

Here Sir Eustace de Hacche made a permanent mark on the landscape by enclosing new arable from the waste. In 1287/8 he made an agreement with his neighbour, Sir John d'Abernon, allowing him to enclose 16 acres in Leatherhead parish towards Kingston over which John and his tenants had common rights. This episode must be connected with a complaint in 1293 that Hacche had enclosed 18 acres of scrub there and diverted the roads to Oxshott, Stoke and Kingston. Evidently this diversion produced the layout north of Gutters Bridge (the crossing of the Rye Brook by the Leatherhead-Stoke road), where the roads branched to encircle some 18 acres, immediately west of the moated site.

As a part of these operations Hacche seems to have created, or enlarged, a small village. The inquiry made at Robert Darcy's death in 1343 lists 10 bond-men at Pachenesham, and in c.1380 eight villein tenements, six of 10 acres each and the rest smaller, are recorded north of Gutters Bridge. These must have been partly on land enclosed by Hacche in the late 1280s, and the regularity of the 10-acre holdings suggests a degree of planning. So it seems that the open land between the bridge and Patsom Green once contained a 13th-century 'marginal' settlement. It was on poor soil, servile in status and quickly depopulated after the Black Death.

Rentals of 1418 and 1474/5 are the earliest record of Pachenesham land in the south of the parish. They suggest that most town-centre properties were held of this manor, as were the fields called Oxencroft, Cokele and Tibele. But in 1418 Pachenesham seems to have had only some 90 acres of tenant land in the Common Field; the fact that in 1545 the land at Pachenesham itself was reckoned as three-quarters of the manor emphasises the relative unimportance of the rest.

## Thorncroft

Thorncroft's lordship was of a very different kind. John de Cherburgh sold the manor to a noble family, who in turn sold it to Walter de Merton, Henry III's chancellor, in 1266. Walter used it to endow his 'house of Merton's scholars' at Maldon, which became Merton College, Oxford. The scholars of Merton were in the forefront of 13th-century estate management and they remained lords of Thorncroft until 1904. Hence, through the later Middle Ages the manorial administration was both stable and efficient, producing a splendid series of court rolls and accounts still preserved at Oxford.

Thorncroft manor house lay on or near the site of its 18th-century successor, south of the town near the river. Beside it were the demesne meadows Mermede and Kuchenmede, and stretching westwards up to Hawks Hill the arable enclosures called la Bochard. The detached block on the Ashtead boundary contained the other demesne enclosures: Barnett, Russette, Pyrycroft, Briddesgrave and Holebergh, and Barnett Wood of which remnants survive today. Thorncroft demesne in the Common Field is harder to quantify, but from the amounts of grain sown there annually, and the frequent 'sales of pasture' at named Common Field locations, it was clearly extensive. In 1629 the Common Field seems to have contained about 600 acres of Thorncroft desmesne, and although this must include former tenant holdings which had reverted to the lord, there can scarcely have been much less than some 300 acres in the Middle Ages.

The accounts provide much information about Merton's farming practice, the crops sown, and even such details as the names of two Thorncroft plough-horses: Balle ('Patch') in 1314/15 and Traunches ('Plodder') in 1328/9. Because so much of the demesne lay in separate enclosures, there was considerable flexibility in matters of cropping and rotations. In 1303 a three-course rotation was evidently practised, for the crops growing in each field were to be the same in three years' time. An average of 173 acres of Thorncroft demesne were sown every year. The demesne livestock, recorded in 1346, included three carthorses, five riding horses, 14 oxen, 11 cows and 250 sheep. The impression is of a farm modestly equipped and not big, but run to Merton's usual high standards.

Thorncroft also had extensive tenant holdings, 37 in a list of 1279. Some 10 of these were outliers in Newdigate and Mickleham; others were the enclosures east of the Common Field called Colecrofte, Hameldones, Redelande and Paines Grove, and the homesteads or crofts called Apperley Hill, Wollandesdene and Pinchuns. The rest, in the Common Field, amounted to two virgates, 10 half-virgates, and miscellaneous plots totalling 17½ acres. Since the Thorncroft virgate was estimated at 26 acres (in other words two of the old 13-acre holdings), the Common Field evidently contained about 200 acres of Thorncroft tenant land.

## Randalls

The main demesne of Little Pachenesham lay along the Mole, between Pachenesham and the town. It was broadly identical with the later Randalls estate; fields totalling 113 acres are listed in *c.*1330. Other land of this manor derived from Margaret de Montfichet's grant: Bochard (Bockett Farm) and Aperderle in demesne, and Joyesfeld with about 93 common-field acres in the hands of tenants. Other small enclosures and some houses in the town were

held of various lords including those of Thorncroft and Pachenesham. The whole estate amounted to some 400 acres, and there was also a substantial flock: 172 sheep, 101 ewes, five rams and 50 lambs in 1327. The servants at Little Pachenesham in 1328 were a drover, two shepherds, a man-servant and a maid. John de Leatherhead and his heirs lived in some style; if not on a level with Hacche, Darcy or the scholars of Merton, they were still the aristocrats of their local community.

## The glebe

Another early land-holding was the church glebe. When first founded, the parish church must have been endowed with Thorncroft land. The glebe comprised a block of enclosures south of the church, and common-field land totalling 44 acres when first recorded in 1599. But because of the absentee medieval rectors, it had little direct influence on the life of Leatherhead.

## The Common Field and the commons

Thus the lands of the manors still lay apart except when they were intermixed in the Common Field. Since both the Little Pachenesham and the glebe holdings were originally formed out of Thorncroft, it appears that almost ninety per cent of the common-field land can be traced back to a Thorncroft origin. So the Common Field was not a fusion of manorial interests, but derived from one manor.

## Status, land-holding and manorial discipline

As usual in Surrey, the division of rights between independent manors meant that controls on the individual peasant were relatively light. Since no one manor represented the whole farming township, no one manor court could dictate township custom. Even in the Common Field, private enterprise had much reduced any early rigidity of holdings or services. Nor were rotations and cropping courses imposed by general agreement. The tenants of

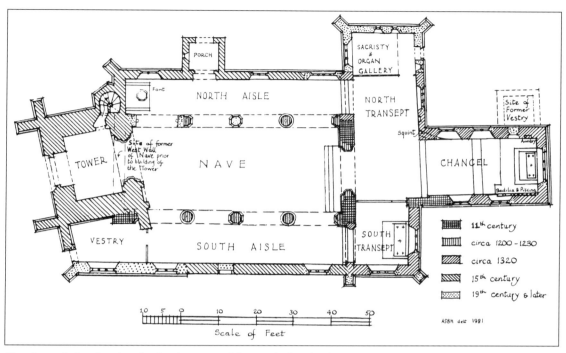

**15** Ground plan showing the development of the parish church of St Mary and St Nicholas through the centuries, drawn by Antony Hill.

strips within each furlong were probably left to agree amongst themselves what crops they would grow from year to year. On all the manors there were more free than villein tenants, and even the villeins were probably in a stronger position than their counterparts in other counties.

It would be wrong to think that manorial discipline was unimportant. All farmers had their land from one or more of the manors and owed something in return. This is why land was assessed in multiples or fractions of the virgate ('yardland' in English), for within each manor all virgates may once have borne similar services. By the 1270s freeholders paid rents which remained fixed thereafter (some of them into the 20th century), but unfree tenants owed labour services as well, and their rents were more fluid. The Thorncroft villeins were one virgater, six half-virgaters and one quarter-virgater, and there were also seven cottagers

holding one acre each. The virgated holdings were burdened with a wide range of agricultural services and building maintenance works, whereas the cottagers' duties were mainly confined to the harvest. On the other manors, services seem to have been light and fading away well before the Black Death. At Little Pachenesham in *c*.1300, Serle le Mouner's villein half-virgate was on the way to emancipation. He owed 2s. rent 'and must find a man in August every day so long as the lord needs to mow, and the lord will find food for him; and all his other services are remitted in return for land of his own which the lord has taken into his hand'. While Merton College applied its standard policy of maintaining labour services, the other lords seem to have been content to relinquish them in return for land or rent.

The lord's will and the custom of the manor were enforced through the manorial court which all tenants were supposed to attend.

The most important official was the reeve, whose office gave him considerable influence in the manor. Between the 1270s and the 1320s the Thorncroft administration was dominated by Simon de Burford, who was frequently reeve, a regular adviser to Merton College, and tenant of the demesne between 1303 and 1306.

### The land market and social change, 1250–1350

By 1300 manorial tenure is a very poor guide to Surrey freeholders' actual wealth and status. An expanding land market had fragmented and recombined the old virgated holdings into farms which owed little to manorial custom.

However, restraints on villein holdings were much greater. Tenants were forbidden to alienate them in whole or part without their lord's consent, which for obvious reasons was rarely granted. But loopholes could be found. In the early 14th century temporary leases of unfree land were regularly made at both Pachenesham and Thorncroft, either officially (in which case a licence fee was charged) or

illicitly (in which case a fine was imposed on discovery), but the actual pattern of occupation may have been very different.

### The families

Some families rose, others fell. Old names such as Punsherst, Oxencroft and Bradmere fade away during the early 14th century. Other old families, the d'Abernons of Stoke, for instance, bought to consolidate existing holdings. The de Aperdeles, leading local men since the 12th century, now seem more important than ever, constantly buying and selling land in association with their Mickleham relatives, the de Newenhams. The early 14th-century John de Aperdele was a royal bailiff and seneschal of Merton College's Surrey manors, and his son was a scholar at Merton. John and Roger de Aperdele were easily the biggest Leatherhead taxpayers in 1332 and Roger's status is emphasised by the perpetual chantry which he founded in Leatherhead church, frustrated after his death through lack of funds. What seems to be this family's swan-song is a grant by William

ROBERTVS CHESEMAN . ANNO . DM .   . ETATIS . SVÆ . XLVIII · M · D · XXXIII ·

**16** After the dissolution of religious houses, Henry VIII allowed his yeoman falconer Robert Cheseman to live in the Mansion, 'Minchin'. Robert was one of 120 squires who met Anne of Cleves when she came to marry the king. He also served on the Grand Jury at the trials of Katherine Howard and Cardinal Wolsey. His portrait is by Hans Holbein the Younger.

Aperdele in 1366 of a house, 38 acres and 13s. 4d. rent in Leatherhead to Kilburn Nunnery, creating the later 'manor of the Minchin'.

Most other names of the 1320s and 1330s are new: Gilbert le Hore, John Hayward, John Faulkes, Gilbert le Glovere, Nicholas Cornmonger, John de Wolvestone, John Payne and many others. They appear time and time again in deeds and court-roll entries, though their families were unknown or of little account before 1280. These men belonged to a new broad yeoman class who were neither gentry nor peasants. They held and farmed land on patterns which they had worked out for themselves and, as well as land, they had draught beasts and large sheep flocks. Even if Leatherhead society had changed much since the early 13th century, it was still notably free and prosperous.

## After the Black Death

Economic history, unlike political history, has few precise dates; but one is the late summer of 1348 when bubonic plague arrived in England. The first and most savage epidemic, the Black Death of 1348-50, killed a third of the inhabitants of England. Later attacks reduced the population to something like half its pre-plague level by 1377, and no long-term recovery came until the 1460s. So for over a century labour was scarce, wages high and prices stagnant. Effects on the landscape and its exploitation were profound. Landlords had to adjust to a harder world, while better opportunities opened up for the more fortunate peasants.

## Removal of direct seigneurial control

A trend which did affect Leatherhead was the withdrawal of manorial lords from direct control of their demesne lands. As labour problems grew, estate management ceased to be worth the bother. It was easier to negotiate a reasonable yearly rent with a local man who could tackle the problems on the spot and reap the rewards, if any, of his diligence. Thus the aristocrat of late medieval village society was

**17** Sir Ivo Fitzwarren, 1414, a brass on the north chapel wall of Wantage Church, Berkshire.

the yeoman with enough cash to take on such a lease and become a 'demesne farmer'.

At Pachenesham the story is one of discord and dereliction. Care may have been poor during Robert Darcy's later years, since at his death in 1343 the manor house was said to be 'worth nothing', and it seems that the demesne was already leased out by 1347 to Roger de Aperdele. Darcy's heir was his son-in-law Sir John d'Argentein, succeeded in 1383 by his own son-in-law Sir Ivo Fitzwarren. In 1386

Fitzwarren and his wife leased the manor house and demesne for 20 years to one William Wimbledon, a newcomer who was to build up wide local interests.

This was a mistake for, like many such tenants, Wimbledon had no links with the manor and his interests were purely financial. In 1393 he defaulted on the rent and the Fitzwarrens claimed that he had dismantled a hall, two chambers, a chapel, two barns, two watermills, two byres, a hay-house and a dove-cote to sell the timber, and had felled 110 trees. Whether or not he should be blamed for the destruction of the manor house, it had been reduced to a mere 'site' by the time of Fitzwarren's death in 1414.

After the Wimbledon affair the Pachenesham demesne was divided up piece-meal between 12 lessees, ceasing to exist as a working farm until 1494/5, when it seems to have been leased as a unit. With a series of absentee lords and without a manor house, Pachenesham manor can have meant little to the people of 15th-century Leatherhead.

The Little Pachenesham family survived into the 15th century, though John Randolf himself died in 1349 (presumably of plague) leaving his son William, then a minor. By 1383 William had leased the Bockett Farm demesne to Nicholas Slyfield although he kept direct control of the fields around his house at Pachenesham. The Randolfs seem to have had lawless tendencies. In 1380 William was out-lawed for an armed robbery at Oxford, and some thirty years later his heir Nicholas Randolf was accused of menacing one Lawrence West so that he feared for his life.

Most other pre-plague families—even the Aperdeles—had vanished from the Leatherhead scene by 1400. In 1392 Ranulph Higden recorded in his chronicle a fire which consumed almost the whole town.

### The new gentry families

Leading families of Tudor and Stuart Leatherhead start to appear during the 15th century. Most seem to begin with outsiders who bought their way in piecemeal, gradually acquiring holdings on the various manors. The Pachenesham rentals of 1418, 1474/5 and 1509 show a tendency for old smallholdings to become progressively more concentrated into fewer gentry hands. Thus William Wimbledon founded a family which, though based at Norbury Park in Mickleham, appear regularly as Thorncroft and Pachenesham tenants until 1498 when his great-grandson's inheritance passed to the Stydolfs. Thereafter the Stydolfs became more and more important in Leatherhead, and had acquired the whole lord-ship of Pachenesham by Queen Elizabeth's reign. Other familiar names from the years 1450-1530 are John Rypingden (lessee of the Rectory in 1470), John Trevelyan, and John Richardson (lessee of Thorncroft during 1510 and one of the two biggest taxpayers in 1524). The Skeets, who first appear in 1454, had acquired a major interest in Thorncroft and Pachenesham holdings by 1500. The Randolf estate passed eventually to the Sands family of Shere, who were settled at Randalls by the 1540s. Another leading family begins with Walter Rogers, the other biggest taxpayer in 1524 and probably lessee of the Rectory; he may have leased Pachenesham too. Thus the gentry families of Elizabethan Leatherhead grew out of the old order, both as engrossers of small-holdings and as demesne farmers.

### Social change and peasant prosperity

For lesser families too there were wide oppor-tunities. As depopulation left holdings vacant, land became easier to acquire. In the long run, the plague emancipated unfree tenants from the disabilities of their status. Lords found them-selves forced to let vacant villein holdings at simple cash rents, and eventually to remit the services of the villeins themselves. Eventually the term 'villein' was replaced by the more dignified 'copyholder' (meaning that the tenant possessed a copy of the court-roll entry recording his admission). At Pachenesham all

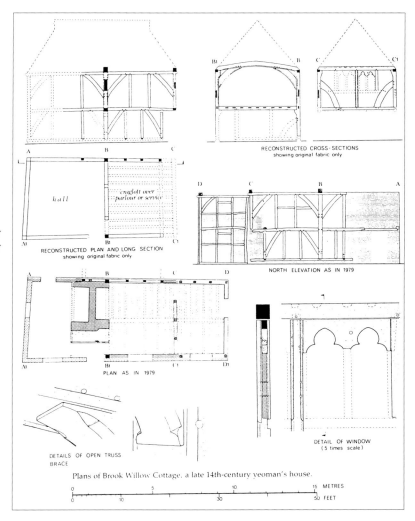

RECONSTRUCTED CROSS-SECTIONS
showing original fabric only

*hall*

*croglott over parlour or service*

RECONSTRUCTED PLAN AND LONG SECTION
showing original fabric only

NORTH ELEVATION AS IN 1979

PLAN AS IN 1979

DETAIL OF WINDOW
(5 times scale)

DETAILS OF OPEN TRUSS
BRACE

Plans of Brook Willow Cottage, a late 14th-century yeoman's house.

| 0 | 5 | 10 | 15 METRES |
| 0 | 10 | 30 | 50 FEET |

**18** Plans of Brook Willow Farm, a late 14th-century yeoman's house, by J. Blair.

labour services had ceased by 1418, and by 1530 the only trace at Thorncroft was the residual duty of a day's harvesting attached to a couple of holdings.

Yeomen and husbandmen had wide freedom in how they farmed their holdings and managed their crops and flocks. One important change was the decay of the bond village at Pachenesham. The destruction of the nearby manor house must have hastened decay. In 1472 a Pachenesham jury found that they had no cucking-stool, and that the pillory, the stocks and the bridge called 'Goodryche bryge' were utterly ruined through the lord's neglect.

Fewer tenants meant more land to go round, and more land meant more cash, hence rich peasants started to live in better houses. A relic of these years is a little timber-framed house at Pachenesham (now Brook Willow Farm Cottage) which must have been built on land of the decaying village. Originally it had an open hall, an enclosed lower room, and a first-floor chamber open to the hall through a massive arched truss. The other end of the chamber was jettied out and had a finely carved window. The carpentry, probably late 14th century, is of a high quality although the planning is by contrast crude, for the upper room must have filled with smoke from the hall fire.

From the late 15th century the population of England rose again and an expanding economy brought new material comforts for all but the poorest. This was the age of the 'Great Rebuilding', when open halls were equipped with chimneys and floored over to provide smoke-free houses and more private rooms.

In 1497 a new timber manor house was built at Thorncroft, and the accounts show that it had two brick chimneys and a 'loft' over the hall. In farmhouses the open hall survived for another generation, as at the *Running Horse*; the cross-wing of 'Rowhurst', Pachenesham may have accompanied such a hall. The Old Vicarage, with an upper chamber jettied over Vicarage Lane, was probably built in these years by Robert Russell, vicar from 1510 to 1557, whose inventory illustrates rising prosperity.

**19**   The Old Vicarage in an 1821 etching by Harriet Dallaway.

*The Vicar of Leatherhead's possessions in 1557*

| | £ | s | d |
|---|---:|---:|---:|
| 3 beds and fittings | £4 | 12 | 8 |
| 2 chests and a counter table | £1 | 0 | 0 |
| 2 chairs and 2 joint stools | | 3 | 4 |
| a gown lined with fox-fur | £2 | 13 | 4 |
| 2 gowns lined | £2 | 0 | 0 |
| 2 jackets and 2 doublets | £1 | 0 | 8 |
| 2 pairs of hose | | 6 | 0 |
| 3 pairs of sheets | | 12 | 0 |
| a diaper table-cloth | | 6 | 0 |
| a table-cloth | | 4 | 0 |
| 2 towels | | 6 | 0 |
| 3 table napkins | | 2 | 0 |
| certain old books | | – | |
| 2 pots | | 13 | 4 |
| 2 pewter pots | | 2 | 4 |
| a brass pot | | 6 | 8 |
| 2 kettles | | 6 | 0 |
| 24 pewter platters, dishes and saucers | | 16 | 0 |
| 2 spits with 'coupe' irons | | 4 | 8 |
| 6 latten candlesticks | | 6 | 0 |
| a salt cellar | | | 6 |
| 11 silver spoons | £1 | 5 | 0 |
| a horse | £1 | 0 | 0 |
| a cow | £1 | 0 | 0 |
| 3 wether sheep | | 10 | 0 |
| 3 ewe sheep | | 7 | 0 |
| cash | £51 | 0 | 0 |
| | £71 | 4 | 2 |

## The late medieval town

Leatherhead has always hovered on the urban borderline, scarcely bigger than such villages as Great Bookham and Cobham, yet marked out as a small town by the special character of its inhabitants and buildings. The town always had a bridge across the Mole. In the 1280s it was said to be maintained 'by the alms of the neighbourhood'. In 1361 alms were being collected for repairing Leatherhead bridge. Today the Georgian brickwork encases the remains of a medieval stone bridge of 14 arches with chamfered vaulting ribs.

The town plan is a simple one based on four main streets meeting at a crossroads. The upper end of North Street, now Gravel Hill, was known throughout the Middle Ages as the 'Berghe' or 'Borough', and tenements are

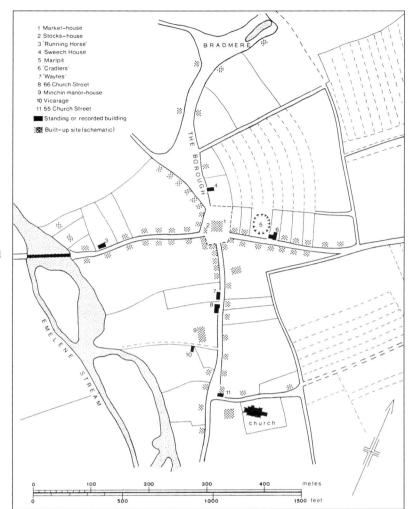

**20** The town centre at the end of the Middle Ages.

recorded here before 1300. Further north, at the foot of Bull Hill, was Bradmere, home of the family of that name. Southwards, the built-up area extended as far as Church Road.

The house-plots on the north side of the High Street are strikingly regular. The block may have originated as a Common Field furlong containing 13 slightly curved strips of equal width, adapted in the medieval town to make a series of regular tenements fronting on the street. In at least five cases the house and garden were held in the early post-medieval period by the same tenant as the Common Field acre strip abutting its northern end. Most of these

plots had houses, but a marlpit (the Swan Pit, obliterated in 1980 by the shopping centre) occupied two tenements' width on the street frontage. This may have been the same 'marlyngput' which faced a house held of Pachenesham manor in 1418. By 1629 the pit was disused and contained the common sheep pens. Marl (chalk) was vital for farmers to enrich the often heavy local soils.

**The market place**

The medieval market place was at the central crossroads, perhaps with buildings set back at the street corners and grouped around it. In

**21**    A watercolour by Hassell of the stocks house in 1822 showing the lock-up at the side known as 'the cage'.

1673 John Aubrey wrote that the market 'hath been discontinued now about an hundred yeares. The Markett house was remayning here within these fifty yeares'. By analogy with other small towns, this market house was probably late medieval and built in an existing open market place. It seems the most likely explanation for the peculiar staggering of the central crossroads. Post-medieval infilling might have incorporated a previously free-standing hall at the present High Street–North Street corner, thus causing Church Street and North Street to be offset in relation to each other. Elias Allen's map of 1629 does show an exceptionally large building on this site, against which the *Swan Inn* seems to have been built.

Two other public buildings appear in late medieval sources. The stocks house, first mentioned in 1418, was a small free-standing building in the market place. It appeared on the 1629 and 1783 maps and was rebuilt in brick in the 17th century. A reference in 1509 to 'a plot of land next le Chirchehall' reveals the existence of a communal hall for meetings and festivities such as 'parish ales'. Common in medieval England, such halls often disappeared at the Reformation, and in Leatherhead even the site has been lost.

**Farmhouses and shops**

The town seems to have contained a mixture of farmhouses and shops. On the one hand, yeomen farming in and around Leatherhead often lived in the town. Thus in 1414 Merton College leased its holding by Leatherhead bridge to John Cradler, who was to build an adequate house there within 18 months. On the other hand, late medieval sources mention shops. There was one on the Bridge Street–Church Street corner in 1280, and at about the same date Gilbert Sutor granted a shop in Leatherhead between houses of Thomas Messor and Henry le Polere. A shop 'next the cross of Leatherhead', formerly held by John le Chapman, is mentioned in 1319. 'Newly built corner shops' in le Chirchelane (Church Road) were held of Pachenesham in 1418, and the same rental mentions an empty plot formerly built on with a tenement and shop.

Of surviving buildings, much the most interesting is 33/35 High Street ('Cradlers'), a copyhold of Thorncroft. Carpentry details in its timber frame suggest a 14th-century date. The main range, at right-angles to the street, is of three bays: perhaps a shop on the frontage, a service room in the middle, and a kitchen or private hall behind. Upstairs was a big two-bay chamber; a smaller one at the back covered half the hall-kitchen, leaving the other half open for smoke from the fire to rise to an outlet in the roof. At right-angles to the main range, along the street frontage, was another open hall. As well as this unusual provision of two halls, the alignment of the main range suggests a distinctively urban need to make best use of the precious frontage.

55 Church Street (on the corner of Church Road) is also set end-on to the main street, over which it is jettied. It is of two bays, spanned upstairs by an open truss. This may simply be the cross-wing of a destroyed open hall, but there remains the interesting possibility that it repeats the primitive form of Brook Willow Farm Cottage: a hall behind, open both to the roof and to a chamber over the front bay. Perhaps there was also a shop on the ground floor. Given its location, this might be one of the 'newly built corner shops' of 1418.

The *Running Horse* in Bridge Street, built on glebeland of Leatherhead church, has a rather squat open hall aligned on the street and spanned by a moulded truss. The two-bay cross-wing, jettied over the street, has an impressive upper chamber with an open truss matching the hall. It seems unlikely that the *Running Horse* was built as an inn: to all appearances it is a high-quality private house of 1450-1550.

At Sweech House, Gravel Hill, the south range seems to be a complete small house, with smoke blackening in the roof as evidence for an open hall. This too was aligned end-on to the street, perhaps recalling a time when the east side of the 'Borough' was built up like an urban frontage. So if only 'Cradlers' is distinctively urban, all these four buildings are, for various reasons, slightly different from ordinary village houses.

**22**  A romanticised view of the *Running Horse* by Harriet Dallaway.

**23**  The *Running Horse* early in the 20th century. This was once presumed to be the inn of Elinour Rumming, immortalised in the 16th century in a ballad by John Skelton which was set to music centuries later by Ralph Vaughan Williams.

**24**  Sweech House on Gravel Hill in 1902, showing shops and the clock tower.

## Craftsmen, tradesmen and farmers

Identifying the people is less easy. With a complex settlement pattern, it is rarely clear who lived in the town and who in the countryside. For Leatherhead's trades and industry there is no direct evidence, and the only guide is an analysis of the occupational surnames of local people in the 13th and 14th centuries. This is beset with problems as such names were fast becoming hereditary. The overall pattern in Leatherhead does, however, seem significantly different from that in the villages around it. Even if some names were inherited by their 14th-century bearers, they probably reflect genuine local trades of a past generation.

Several occupational names are of the ordinary rural kind: Smith, Baker, Carpenter, Miller and Shepherd. Others, conspicuously absent in surrounding parishes, suggest a greater economic diversity. Skinner, Tanner, Weaver and Fuller on the one hand, and Shoemaker, Clover and Tailor on the other, point to a clothing trade backed up by production of the raw materials. Commerce at the market, and the outside contracts it brought, are reflected in the names of Merchant, Chapman, Cornmonger and Gaveler (moneylender). Poller (barber) also seems more suited to a town than a village. Farmers from the countryside around would come to Leatherhead on market-day, buy their shoes and gloves, and perhaps have their hair cut.

Nor would they forget to visit the town alehouse. Agnes Hostilere, mentioned in 1383, presumably kept a hostelry. A much more celebrated Leatherhead ale-wife was the redoubtable Elinour Rumming. John Skelton's comic poem, written in the first quarter of the 16th century, describes her grotesque appearance and the riotous scenes in her tavern. Elinour was a genuine local character. In 1525 she was fined 2d. in the Pachenesham manor court for selling ale at excessive prices. Exactly where she sold it is, however, unknown (there

is no real evidence to associate her with the *Running Horse*). What may have been another hostelry, a tenement in Leatherhead called 'le George', is mentioned in 1543.

Taxation records give a rough measure of the importance of Leatherhead and its wealthier inhabitants in relation to other places around. Unfortunately there is nothing between the Lay Subsidy return of 1332 and that of 1524, and even these exclude many householders, perhaps the majority, whose goods fell below a minimum value. In 1332 the 54 taxpayers certainly exceeded any neighbouring parishes (49 in Ewell, 35 in Mickleham, 29 in Fetcham and 28 in Ashtead), while the average value of goods assessed per taxpayer (£32 10s. in Leatherhead, £32 in Ewell and lesser sums in Mickleham, Fetcham and Ashtead) points to somewhat greater prosperity in possessions and stock. If most of these people lived in the town, the basic farming population was evidently swelled by craftsmen and tradesmen with sufficient material resources to qualify as taxpayers. In 1524 Leatherhead's 65 taxpayers still substantially exceeded Mickleham (28), Fetcham (20) and Ashtead (37), though were now surpassed by Ewell (70). A breakdown of the figures suggests that both Leatherhead and Ewell had unusually large numbers of humbler taxpayers with goods valued at £1.

Medieval Leatherhead was unequivocally a small town, with shops and a market to serve the interests of craftsmen, tradesmen and farmers. A 1418 reference to an empty plot formerly containing a shop may be the first hint of a slow decline in commercial functions and the 1524 tax returns show the town already overshadowed by the rapid growth of Ewell. Soon afterwards the ancient market ceased to be held and the market-place disappeared. So Leatherhead was more obviously a town in the 14th century than in the 16th when its early promise seemed unfulfilled.

## Chapter Four

# The Elizabethan and Stuart Period 1558–1714

Leatherhead was a busy little town at this period. Although still mainly a farming community, courtiers and city merchants became commuters and made their home there. Edmund Tylney, Master of the Revels to Queen Elizabeth, was visited by her in 1591 at The Mansion while Robert Gardiner, Sergeant of the Wine Cellar early in her reign, lived nearby at Thorncroft Manor.

Edmund Tylney was also the Censor and sole publisher of most performance plays. So it is likely that Shakespeare visited him and may have named Verges, an officer of the watch in *Much Ado About Nothing*, after Leatherhead's constable, George Varges. In his *Bartholomew Fair* Ben Johnson named a puppeteer 'Lanthorn Leatherhead', presumably a satirical dig at the powerful Censor.

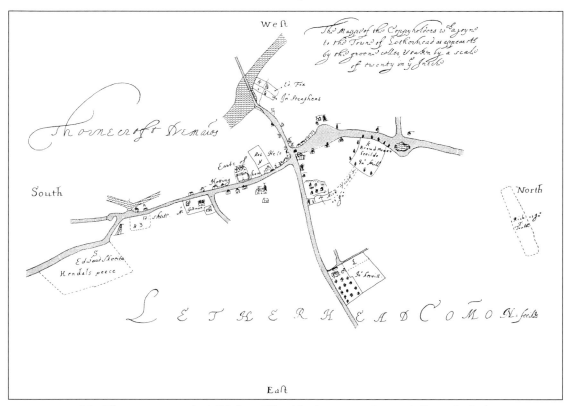

**25**　The town centre in 1629 from Elias Allen's survey, Merton College, Oxford.

**26** A token minted for Edward Shales, the innkeeper of the *Swan*.

**27** Sergeant of the wine cellar Robert Gardiner's helmet, now in the parish church, was restored by Claude Blair of the V & A. Gardiner's epitaph by a minor Court poet, Thomas Churchyard, also hangs in the church.

Other notable residents were the Earl of Nottingham, who was Lord Lieutenant of Surrey; a member of the Long Parliament, Thomas Sands of Randalls Park; a mercantile family Godman, and the Rogers who lived at the Rectory and farmed the church's glebeland.

In the late 17th century Richard Dalton, Sergeant of the Wine Cellar to Charles II, lived here, followed by his son who held the same post. Dalton was a friend of Samuel Pepys, who noted disparagingly in his diary that, during the Great Fire of London, the Lord Mayor Sir Thomas Bludworth panicked. Bludworth lived most of his life at Thorncroft Manor, dying there in 1682. His daughter married Judge Jeffreys, known as 'the Hanging Judge' because of his harsh treatment of the Monmouth rebels in 1685.

## The growing town and its occupations

Shortly prior to Elizabeth's reign, the lay subsidy returns of 1524/5 estimated Leatherhead had 300 inhabitants, and by 1603, the year of her death, it had grown to 394. By the end of the 17th century there were about 700 inhabitants, in spite of epidemics like influenza and typhus in 1660 and 1680. No doctors were listed but, from a monument in the parish church, it seems a surgeon-apothecary lived in the town and died in 1726.

In a corn-growing area with cattle, sheep and horses, it is not surprising to find a miller in the town, an oatmeal maker and a maltster, with blacksmiths, carpenters and turners, tanners, cloth workers, butchers, bakers and brewers. By 1661 there was added a fishmonger, a wheelwright, a glazier and at least two bricklayers. The only craftsmen of that period who can be named were the Ragge family who made padded leather collars and saddles for horses. They lived and worked in Bridge Street and continued in Leatherhead well beyond this century; indeed their descendants still live in the area.

## Civil War

On a June day in 1642 Sir Poynings More, Sir Robert Parkhurst and Nicholas Stoughton, Deputy Lieutenants of Surrey, rode into Leatherhead to attend a meeting at The Mansion, the home of the Lord Lieutenant of the county, Charles Howard, Earl of Nottingham. The meeting was called to discuss the 'proper ordering' of the county militia at a time of tension between King and Parliament. The county leaders met there again in August 'to settle the county in a posture of arms (for Parliament)'. Urgent decisions had to be made in a increasingly dangerous political atmosphere and only a few days later Charles I raised his standard at Nottingham. The Civil War had begun.

Less than two months after the Civil War started the Earl of Nottingham died, but Leatherhead maintained a link with the outside world through Thomas Sands of Randalls Park, who had been elected to the Long Parliament as one of the members for Gatton, near Reigate. He supported the Parliamentary cause like most Surrey members, and Leatherhead probably followed his example, although some families like the Gardiners and the Rogers were staunchly Royalist.

For a time, local people went about their business with little concern for the comings and goings at The Mansion and Randalls Park. They were not involved in any of the armed confrontations which took place in the Thames Valley in 1642, though some Leatherhead men may have been part of the Earl of Essex's army inconclusively facing King Charles and Prince Rupert at Turnham Green in November that year.

## Royalist troops at The Mansion (September 1643)

Many months after Cavalier activity had been curbed in Surrey, there were reports of Royalist troops making their presence felt in various parts of the county including Leatherhead, encouraged perhaps by the Royalist successes against Parliament in the summer of 1643. Some of the King's soldiers appeared in Leatherhead on the night of 18 September 1643 and broke into The Mansion where the widowed Countess of Nottingham was living. Nothing more is known about the affair but the troops were soon rounded up.

## The Leatherhead Mutiny (February 1645)

In the two years after the incident at The Mansion, Parliament achieved success in the two decisive battles of Marston Moor (July 1644) and Naseby (June 1645). It was between these battles, in February 1645, that an episode occurred in Leatherhead which was more than locally important. By 1644 the victory of Marston Moor had been dimmed by the Earl of Essex's defeat in Cornwall, by the inconclusive second battle of Newbury and by disaffection among Sir William Waller's troops. Many of them had deserted because of pay arrears and dislike of campaigning far from home. All this led Parliament to consider forming a New Model Army which would be better disciplined, better trained and more regularly paid. The House of Commons agreed in January 1645 and the House of Lords' acceptance was hastened because the Leatherhead incident showed 'it would be impossible to carry on with a disorganised army'. Waller had been ordered to relieve Weymouth in early February 1645, but delays occurred because his cavalry, formerly part of the Earl of Essex's army, and some infantry had mutinied at Leatherhead. This was discussed by the Committee of Both Kingdoms in London on 15 February, Cromwell being one of its members, and it reported to the House of Commons.

**28 & 29**  Major-General Skippon (left) was sent to quell the mutiny in Leatherhead against Sir William Waller (right).

Indiscipline among Waller's troops was not new, for a few months previously he had complained to London about it; this had even reached the ears of the Venetian ambassador who reported on 18 November 1644 that Waller had 'fallen into the lowest estimation with his soldiers'.

Two of the leading Parliamentary generals, Balfour and Skippon, were ordered down to Leatherhead to quell the mutiny. Sir William Balfour had fought at Edgehill and was a renowned cavalry officer; Skippon was also an experienced general, being appointed about this time second-in-command to Fairfax in the New Model Army. The House of Commons was most concerned about the Leatherhead affair and ordered Cromwell to report on it to them. The number of horse and foot troops involved in the mutiny is thought to have been about 700, a considerable body of soldiers, and their presence in and around Leatherhead created a

large stir, not least because of the arrival in the district of the two generals under Cromwell's orders. After the troops finally left for the west under Sir William Waller and Cromwell himself, Leatherhead became quiet until the end of the Civil War, which followed the taking of the King's headquarters at Oxford in June 1646.

**The troubled peace (1646–48)**

The end of the first Civil War in 1646 was followed by disagreements among the victors about how the country should be run. Leatherhead people were soon disillusioned since they and others throughout the country suffered two bad harvests in 1646 and 1647 and the price of wheat soared to record heights. Much of the blame for the high cost of living was put on the government. There were also complaints that too many units of the New Model Army continued in Surrey, even though the war was over, and that the soldiers' demands for free quarters and supplies were unreasonable. Plans were made to petition Parliament.

The first of several meetings held to draw up the Surrey petition was held in Leatherhead on 2 May 1648 when great numbers came to the town from all over the county. They recommended that there should be a 'Personal Treaty between His Majesty and Parliament'; that 'the Armies may be disbanded'; and that 'the Arrears of the Armies may be satisfied and paid'. The submission to Parliament was made on 16 May by a large body of Surrey men, resulting in an affray with soldiers on guard at the House as well as some fatalities.

Parliament could hardly have been expected to accept in full the Surrey petitioners' requests, but Fairfax was instructed that if any of his forces passed through the county, they should 'take care to carry themselves inoffensively to the people'. So the petition had some success.

### The second Civil War (1648)

A few weeks before the excitement of the Surrey petition the second Civil War had started with a rising in Wales and soon spread elsewhere. Kent took up arms for the King late in May and Essex followed soon after. Surrey and Sussex joined a month later. The Surrey rising was small and poorly organised starting early in July 1648 and lasting only a few days.

On Thursday 6 July 1648, Leatherhead was disturbed as some 500 to 600 troops mainly on horseback passed through the town on their way to Dorking. They had ridden from Kingston and formed the chief part of the Earl of Holland's Royalist forces, assembled a day or two previously in the hope that strong support would come from the county. This did not happen and the small force moved south hoping to join up with Sussex rebels. But, after reaching Reigate, they immediately retreated to Dorking as Parliamentary troops approached under Sir Michael Livesey. On 7 July the Royalists retreated, once again passing through Leatherhead, pursued by Livesey's men. There was a small skirmish at Ewell, another at Nonsuch and

the Royalists finally turned on their pursuers at Surbiton only to be thoroughly defeated.

### The Interregnum (1649-60)

It is not known how Leatherhead people reacted to the trial and execution of Charles I, the abolition of the House of Lords and the formation of the Commonwealth in early 1649. They would certainly have known that Thomas Sands of Randalls Park had returned to Leatherhead after being excluded from Parliament by Pride's Purge in December 1648.

Leatherhead people were probably less concerned with the goings on in London than with the recent bad harvest, the fourth in a row, which caused rocketing food prices. So there may have been a little sympathy for the short-lived Diggers' movement led by Gerard Winstanley at St George's Hill, Weybridge, which in April 1649 bravely claimed the right to dig and grow food on common land. However, a series of good harvests in the 1650s helped the return to stable living conditions after years of disruptive war.

### Farming in a changing world (1558-1660)

Elizabeth came to the throne in the year the harvest throughout the country was the best for many years, so the new reign started well in the farmers' eyes and it was not until the 1590s that there was a run of poor harvests. Social and economic pressures started to lead to changes in farming.

Among the factors for change was the growth of Leatherhead's population, like that of other towns. The extra food needed had to be produced by increasing crop yields, especially in wheat, and by extending the cultivated areas. Books were being published on how to improve the soil and those by Tusser, Googe and Norden were most widely read. Writing on the eve of the Civil War, Fuller colourfully describes how the yeoman of the day 'improveth his land to a double value by his good husbandrie—some grounds that wept with water or frowned with thorns, by draining the one and cleansing the other, he makes both to laugh and sing with corn'.

The change in farming habits was gradual and for most the traditional ways seemed to be the best. In the year of Queen Elizabeth's death, fear of the plague added to farmers' worries and trade suffered. This did not last long because the following year saw the end of the war with Spain which, for the wealthier farmers, like Sir Francis Stydolf and the Sands family of Randalls Park, meant a release from some of the burdens of taxation. A run of good harvests in the next three years increased their prosperity.

During the whole of James I's reign there were only four poor harvests. The year 1620 came to be remembered as having the most abundant crop returns since Elizabeth came to the throne. There was then a sudden swing to harder conditions, made worse in 1625 by another serious plague. Farming continued to be depressed over much of Charles I's reign up to the outbreak of the Civil War, due mainly to a fall in wool prices.

The Leatherhead Common Field lay on the lower slopes of the Downs, like those at Fetcham and Great Bookham and other parishes along the north-facing chalk hills. It was divided into strips, each individually owned. Shown in detail on the Gwilt map of Leatherhead (1782/3), there were 374 strips in all including six in the extension to the Common Field called the Common Fair Field, north of what is now the High Street.

The Common Meadow along the river near the Leatherhead bridge and the 'open' Downs well to the south were important to farming at this time, providing hay and pasturage for livestock. The manor courts exercised strict control over their use as they did over the common 'waste' on the northern limits of the parish.

Wheat, barley, peas and beans were the main crops grown. In 1595 'the north side of the Downes between Guildford and Leatherhead' was described as one of the 'greatest places for corne' in Surrey. About this time Robert Sands bequeathed to his son '10 acres in winter wheat, now sown in Leatherhead', while Edward Skeete, another local farmer in Elizabeth's reign, left barley to his children and servants.

Wheat was used by wealthy farmers and gentry mainly to make bread and it was the chief crop sold at the markets. Among the less well off, barley was the staple corn for bread-making, together with rye, though wheat mixed with rye (maslin) was popular as well. Malt and beer were also made from barley. Other crops cultivated may have included hops, since Surrey's 'lowe and spongie ground' was said to be suitable for it. Woad used as a cloth dye was grown. The loss of the market in the middle of Elizabeth's reign may indicate some fall in local trading but Dorking market was not far away. An annual fair was held in the town tradition-ally after the end of the harvest in early August, but in the late 17th century it was said to have taken place on Lady Day.

**Livestock**

Livestock were allowed to use the arable fields only after the harvest (early August); at other times they used the common 'wastes' and in July, after the hay harvest, the riverside meadows. Pasturing rights are referred to in a claim for extending them early in 1610.

The Lower Common, meadow land for 'Great Cattell' along the Mole north of the town, was subdivided into individually owned strips and only thrown open to the whole community after haymaking early in July. The Upper Common, or Leatherhead Downs, high above the town, was for sheep only and there were no limits on the numbers kept there.

**Wastes and woodlands**

Many of the farmers' needs, like wood for fuel, fences and implements, were obtained from the wastes and woodlands of the Leatherhead Downs and the common land adjoining Ashtead, north of the town. Permission had to be sought from the manor courts to cut timber.

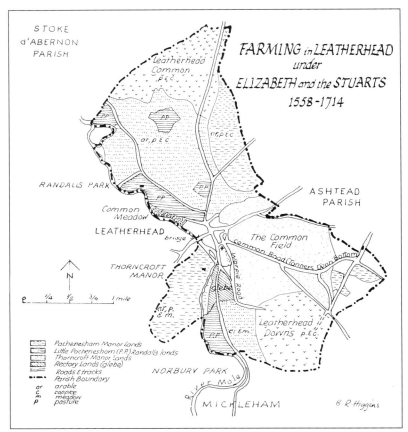

FARMING in LEATHERHEAD
under
ELIZABETH and the STUARTS
1558-1714

Leatherhead
Common
p & c

pp

ar, p & c

ar, p & c

ASHTEAD
PARISH

RANDALLS PARK

pp

pp

Common
Meadow

LEATHERHEAD

bridge

The Common
Field

Common Road Tanners Dean Bottom

Warple Road

THORNCROFT
MANOR

N

¼  ½  ¾  1 mile

ar, p.
& m.

glebe

glebe

c & m

Leatherhead
Downs p & c

P.P.

Pachenesham Manor Lands
Little Pachenesham (P.P.) Randalls lands
Thorncroft Manor Lands
Rectory Lands (Glebe)
Roads & tracks
Parish Boundary
ar    arable
c     coppice
m    meadow
p     pasture

NORBURY PARK

River Mole

MICKLEHAM

B. R. Higgins

**30** Farming in Leatherhead, 1558-1714.

As in the earlier years of the 17th century, the Leatherhead manorial courts concentrated on maintaining common rights without imposing mandatory controls on what crops should be grown in the open arable field. The court records show in particular the pressure to increase the cultivable area by encroaching on common land. At the Pachenesham Manor court of 17 October 1706, three people were fined for enclosing part of Leatherhead Common and this kind of case appears often in other court records. The fines do not seem to have discouraged the encroachers since at subsequent courts the same offenders reappear. Other misdemeanours controverting the manorial rules included allowing cattle and sheep to feed on the meadows or common fields at the wrong times and removing bushes and stakes from Leatherhead Common.

**New ventures in farming**

The urge to cultivate more land was accompanied by an increasing interest in new ways to improve crop yields and provide extra for live-stock. For many years farmers had been pressed to improve their manuring of the soil and to introduce fodder crops like clover, sainfoin and lucerne. Some clover was said to be sown in most counties of England at this time but it was probably not yet widely used as a rotation crop. Farmers in the Leatherhead area seem to have started to grow this new crop since a 1693 inventory refers to a 'parcel of clover' in the barn and the Pachenesham Court records for 29 September 1711 say that 'no persons shall bring their sheep upon any clover or other seed grass after Christmas Day'. The new husbandry also encouraged the production of root crops, especially turnips, which agricultural writers of the day argued would enable the farmer to feed his cattle and sheep throughout the winter.

### The Church in the community (1558–1642)

Leatherhead's parish life followed the ordered course it had always done, determined by the festivals of the Christian year coinciding so often with the seasonal round in farm and field. Yet there were alterations made in church practices in the years before Elizabeth became Queen. Many of the ancient rites had been abolished, the church fabric shorn of its images, walls defaced and vestments sold, although a brief reversal to the old customs had occurred in Mary's reign.

At the time of Elizabeth's accession in November 1558, the vicar of Leatherhead, William Walkeden, had been incumbent for little over a year and he seems to have accepted the abrupt introduction once again of the Protestant faith, first by the need to subscribe to the Acts of Uniformity and Supremacy and then by agreeing to implement the Queen's Injunctions on the correct church practices. The Prayer Book in English was used, and homilies were to be read in church 'every Sunday at the least'. Announced beforehand by the tolling of a bell, litanies and prayers had to be said on Wednesdays and Fridays. The 'holy table' was to be placed in the chancel during the communion service and the clergy were expected to wear 'seemly dress', avoid alehouses and not play cards or dice. It is unlikely that William Walkeden managed to obey all the 1559 injunctions. Sermons, as distinct from homilies, could be delivered only by licensed preachers and the vicar of Leatherhead was not one of these. Therefore he had to read the dreary homilies (even if some were written by Cranmer) Sunday by Sunday; to do otherwise, would have risked the Bishop's wrath. However, since almost the whole bench of Bishops had resigned over Elizabeth's religious

**31** Medieval chest in the parish church once used to store vestments and other precious church valuables. It was protected by the rector and two churchwardens, who held the only keys.

**32**   The Slyfield chest with the date 1663 in brass studs on the lid.

policy, there was a breathing space of a year or two.

It was in 1561 that William Walkeden resigned his Leatherhead living. His resignation suggests an increasing disenchantment brought to a head perhaps by the impending Bishop of Winchester's Visitation. On the whole, the Bishop found Surrey a conforming county. Walkeden had recently married, presumably under Elizabeth's recent dispensation, but if he had not sought permission for this he would have courted disfavour. At all events, no other vicar of Leatherhead took this step, Simon Tysse and John Vaughan dying in office. In 1584, Vaughan was said to be 'a common resorter to alehouses' and given to 'typling and gusling'; one day he had to be 'led home' because of drinking too much. Richard Levitt, who succeeded Vaughan, stayed on until the Civil War.

Church life continued in its routine way. On Sundays, morning service started at nine o'clock and everyone had to attend, defaulters paying one shilling to church funds, which was a large sum in those days. The service lasted about two hours and there was another service in the afternoon and after this the vicar had to catechise the children for perhaps an hour to educate them as best he could.

Vestry meetings were held regularly at the church and much day-to-day business was transacted in the church porch. As in the modern parish, fund-raising was a constant preoccupation of the churchwardens and, although the church rates levied on all householders helped, reliance was partly placed on what were called 'church-ales', lively social gatherings usually held about Whitsuntide. Ale was specially brewed, great quantities of food prepared and minstrels and morris dancers performed during the feasting which might have lasted several days. Close to Whitsuntide, there was the annual perambulation or 'beating of the bounds' of the parish, ending perhaps with a vestry dinner.

None of these activities helped the vicar to improve his lot and he had to depend on a meagre income from the diocese, reduced by compulsory state subsidy payments from time to time, and supplemented only by fees, tithes and perhaps the sale of some farm produce.

The fear of Catholic resurgence and of Protestant extremism common throughout the country in Elizabeth's reign, does not appear to have disturbed Leatherhead. The Archdeaconry of Surrey Returns in 1603 mention only one Catholic living in the town but the three other non-communicants listed may have been members of one of the several extreme Protestant sects like the Brownists or the Barrowists.

## Church and parish during the Civil War and Interregnum

At the outbreak of the Civil War there were few Leatherhead parishioners who could remember a time when Richard Levitt was not their vicar, since by that time he had been so for over 50 years. He was then an old man in his mid-eighties and almost certainly resented the revolutionary religious changes introduced in the 1640s. There had been a foretaste of things to come as early as May 1641, when he and other country vicars had had to obtain from all 18-year-olds and over their signed promise to defend the 'true Reformed Protestant Religion against all Poperie ... and also maintain the power and privileges of Parliament'. This was the so-called Protestation Oath.

More was to follow to disturb the old vicar. He may have approved the call for better observation of Sunday worship, but not its rigid exclusion of all sports and pastimes on Sunday. In January 1645 the Book of Common Prayer, which he and his parishioners had used all their lives, was replaced by the Directory of Public Worship. Christmas and other Feast Days were abolished and heavy fines imposed for non-compliance.

Richard Levitt was replaced as vicar in 1647 by Thomas Mell. It would be wrong to assume that the Presbyterian influence of Thomas Mell or that of itinerant preachers affected deeply the life of the town, which in the Interregnum period had a population of about four hundred. The parish church was still the centre of Leatherhead society and the abolition of penalties for not going to Sunday services contributed to a greater freedom, even though sports and pastimes were still barred. The ban on festivals, especially Christmas, was strongly disliked but private celebrations were probably carried on at home. These were enlivened by music and dancing since these, although both were frowned upon in public, were not discouraged absolutely. Cromwell himself was known to like music and encouraged composers.

The social change possibly most resented in the 1650s was the introduction of civil marriages. After 29 September 1653 Thomas Mell was not allowed to solemnise weddings in the church. These were to take place before Justices of the Peace and a parish official called a Registrar who recorded marriages, births and deaths.

## Church and parish after the Restoration

The Presbyterian vicar of Leatherhead, Thomas Mell, may have thought that radical changes in church life would be avoided in the early months after the Restoration of Charles II, who seemed to favour a Presbyterian-Anglican compromise. This was not to be. In a short time the High Church clergy secured, with Clarendon's help, a full return to Anglican ways: the Act of Uniformity (1662) required all incumbents to follow the Church of England rubric and to use the Common Prayer Book at services. Those who refused to comply were to be ejected from their living. Mell stayed on in Leatherhead until his death in 1671, so he clearly decided to conform.

Leatherhead people readily accepted the return to the traditional Anglican rites. Everyone had to attend church on Sundays as laid down in a proclamation of 22 August 1662 and fines were imposed for non-attendance. Feast days and Anglican Communion were restored and the services were brighter than they had been before the Restoration. Bells rang out and bellringers were busy. The Leatherhead churchwarden's accounts refer to payment of £1 7s. for ringing on 5 November 1712, 6 February and 8 March 1713 with news of peace. Accession bells on 29 May 1713 and bells for the Queen's birthday on 25 January 1714 were rung for which the ringers were paid 6s. on each occasion.

Shortly before the Glorious Revolution in 1688, James II's Chancellor, the notorious Judge Jeffreys, came to Leatherhead to see his dying daughter. In late November that year he sent his family to The Mansion, the home of Sir Thomas Bludworth, to avoid the mounting troubles in London. He is believed to have come here after being told of his daughter's serious illness and probably stayed until her death and burial on 2 December. Legend has it that Jeffreys came to Leatherhead in flight from London rioters and went into hiding 'in an underground chamber' at The Mansion. There seems to be no truth in this; nevertheless the legend has been repeated many times since it was first mentioned by Manning

**33** Judge George Jeffreys by W. Claret, 1678. His reputation as the 'hanging judge', due to his harsh sentencing of the Monmouth rebels, has recently been attributed to his suffering from kidney stones.

and Bray and by Dallaway in the early 19th century.

## Watch and ward by the Vestry

Local disputes and matters of tenure had been regulated by the manorial courts. However, from the 16th century the Tudor statutes, including the Elizabethan Poor Law, placed the responsibility for administration squarely on the parishes. Vestry meetings took over the handling of local matters which were meticulously recorded in Vestry Books dated from 1693-1739.

The vestry, formed from leading parishioners under the vicar, played a central part in Leatherhead's parish life. There were two churchwardens, a constable, two overseers of the poor and two surveyors of the highways. These officials were elected yearly and had to ensure that the church services were properly attended, the church kept clean and tidy and the church rates duly collected.

## Law and order

The constable was responsible for keeping the peace. Though involved with the vestry work, he was elected by the manorial court. In addition, the constable was charged with assembling able-bodied men for musters, collecting taxes and getting rid of rogues and vagabonds. These he often kept in the stocks before sending them on their way with a whipping. The old stocks of Leatherhead probably stood close to the junction of the present North Street with Bridge Street, and in the 17th century there was a building known as the Stocks House near the junction, which may have been a prison.

The records of the Quarter Sessions at this time give the only accurate flavour of the general social scene. By law, people were obliged to attend church, accept fixed wages and sell their produce in markets at fixed prices. They were forbidden to possess certain books, play certain games, whistle or beat a wife after 9 p.m. As well as enforcing these restrictions, the Quarter Sessions dealt with felonies including larceny, witchcraft, the taking of life, rioting, neglect of hedges, pollution of rivers, purse-picking, tippling and immorality. For instance, in 1663 it is recorded that three Leatherhead men, Robert Rowing, labourer, Nicholas Kent, husbandman, and John Munger, wood-breaker, 'threw a great quantity of dung on the highway called Leatherhead Street'. Richard Cottingham 'kept unpruned his hedge against the highway from Leatherhead to Headley'. In 1665 Richard Stone, yeoman, was proclaimed 'a common swearer, evil speaker and profaner of the name of God', while Richard Gardiner was indicted for 'allowing his ditches to overflow'.

Two cases of theft were recorded: one involved the stealing of seven silver spoons from Thomas Bellingham, gent., in 1660, while earlier, in 1595, three towels and several tablecloths were stolen from Edward Skeete by John Harris, a cooper from Buckland. There was more than a breath of scandal in two of the entries. In 1587 Isabel Tenney cut the throat of a baby she had just given birth to in a garden adjacent to the house of her master, John Bramson. She was sentenced to be hanged. In 1602 Anne Woodherst 'conceived and gave birth to two bastards in Leatherhead where she was a servant to Mr Oxenbridge' and the babies were ordered to be supported by the parish. Apart from infanticide, there was only one murder reported. In 1607 a butcher killed another from Mickleham and was duly hanged.

## The poor and needy

Looking after the poor and the sick and handicapped was an important vestry activity, implementing and adding to the central government's Poor Law measures of 1598 and 1601 which have been called the forerunners of National Insurance and were the basis of Poor Law legislation throughout the 17th century. A compulsory poor rate was levied in the parish and overseers of the poor were appointed. Children of poor parents were trained as apprentices. There were donations to seamen, soldiers with passes (distinguishing them from deserters) and 'prisoners from France' passing through Leatherhead at the time of the War of the Spanish Succession. Some were boarded at the Leatherhead almshouse as a charge on the parish.

Private charity was a valuable supplement to the caring work. It was common practice to remember those less fortunate than ourselves in one's wills. Edmund Tylney, Master of the Revels to Queen Elizabeth, and the Earl and Countess of Nottingham left money to the poor. Leatherhead also benefited from charitable trusts. For example, in 1608 John Skeete, a wealthy London merchant, left money for the purchase of land and property, the income from which was to be used for the benefit of the poor of Leatherhead, 'to be distributed in bread ... on every Sunday morning after prayer' by the churchwardens and 'four of the most discreet persons in the parish'. Another generous benefactor was Henry Smith, who it was said was nicknamed 'Dog' Smith, as he had no

**34**   The Rev. Hugh Shortridge DD, rector of Fetcham 1683-1720, whose charitable trust provided for the preaching of a sermon annually on the anniversary of Charles I's execution.

home of his own and dined always at friends' houses. In his will of 24 April 1627 he directed that the churchwardens 'should meet once a month to consider which of the poor should be in most need of relief' offering to them 'bread, flesh or fish on each Sabbath day'. In 1692 Edward Hudson directed that meat should be distributed on feast day evenings to 'twenty of the poorest inhabitants'. Soon after Queen Anne's death more help was forthcoming, this time for the vicar, a yearly sum being left to him and the vicars of Great Bookham, Effingham and Shalford by Dr. Shortridge, the wealthy incumbent resident of Fetcham. In return, prayers were to be said on Wednesdays and Fridays and a sermon preached on Good Friday and on 30 January, the anniversary of Charles I's execution. The money from this trust is still being paid and the sermon is still preached annually in Leatherhead.

Care for the children of the parish extended also to their education and training. Sir Thomas Bludworth's will of 1692 left money for his servant to be trained as an apprentice. The Overseers of the Poor Accounts for 1702 refer to a sum of money being given to 'Goody Harrison for schooling'. There is, however, no record of any true school in Leatherhead at this time, although Pigots' *Directories* of 1832 and 1839 mention a Free School founded and endowed in 1596 for the education of 10 boys. At that time schooling usually took place in church with the parish clerk as schoolmaster. The west tower of the church in Leatherhead bears this out, its walls and columns covered with possibly schoolboy graffiti: names, initials and dates varying from 1662 to 1729.

## Travel and transport

The roads in and around Leatherhead were narrow with rough broken surfaces, dusty in summer and muddy in winter. As early as 1594 these roads were being used for moving goods to London and also to and from Guildford.

In the 1630s there was a regular courier service on Thursdays from Leatherhead to

London, and after the Restoration a stage-wagon or stage-coach on most days of the week took goods, mail and passengers to and from the capital. The roads serving Leatherhead, north to London and south to Dorking, Arundel and Chichester, are shown in J. Ogilby's road survey *Britannia* (1675) and his *Traveller's Road Guide* (1699). Both the wagon and the coach from Leatherhead ended their journey at the *King's Head* in Southwark, as did the services from Epsom, Guildford, Egham, Godalming and Croydon. Despite the growth of wagon and coach services, most travel was by horse. The Vestry Book notes payment for 'horse hire' for journeys to London, Hampton Court and Kingston.

Local farmers and tradesmen carried out their stint of repair work, filling in potholes under the watchful eye of the surveyors of highways who had to report three times a year on the condition of the roads and bridges to the Justices of the Peace. The real improvements to the roads round Leatherhead had to await the Turnpike Acts of the next century and the improved methods of road construction by Telford and McAdam.

## Steps towards a navigable Mole

River navigation, including that of the Mole, was much talked about in the 17th century, especially after Sir Richard Weston's pioneering work in the 1650s making the River Wey navigable from Guildford to the Thames. Parliament passed an Act in April 1662 ordering that all rivers should be made navigable, an over-ambitious scheme which was in practice whittled down to apply only to a few rivers. The Mole, mentioned in an Act of 1664, was to be made 'navigable or passable for barges and other vessels' from Reigate to the Thames. The river's navigability was further advocated in 1698 as the Mole was considered 'fit to be made navigable for vessels of twenty tons burthen' and could transport 'good and vast quantities of timber to build ships ... coals, corn and all other commodities ... to and from London'. More

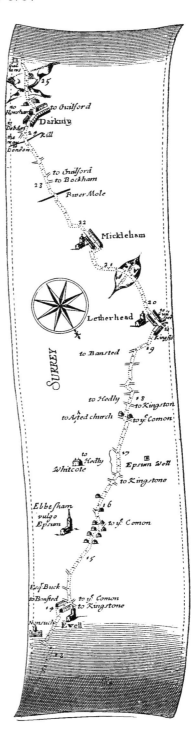

**35**  J. Ogilby's map of the London to Arundel roads (Ewell to Dorking section).

than one survey was made and it was thought Leatherhead's river could rival the Wey, but despite the hopes and recommendations the Mole remained as it had always been.

## The great storm

Early in Queen Anne's reign, Leatherhead and southern England experienced one of the worst storms on record in the country. This was in late November 1703 and it lasted for four to five days, during which time the Eddystone Lighthouse was lost. Daniel Defoe, who wrote about it in a book appropriately entitled *The Storm*, said most people expected 'the fall of their houses' and 'no one thought to venture out'. John Evelyn, in his book *The Pilgrim's Way*, describes the peak of the storm on 26/7 November 1703 when, with little rain and much lightning, the wind caused havoc to his estate at Wotton, near Dorking, where 2,000 oak trees were 'prostrated like whole regiments fallen in battle'. Like very many churches in the south, Leatherhead parish church lost its spire, never to be replaced. The town itself suffered badly, an experience to be repeated nearly three centuries later.

*Chapter Five*

# The Age of the Georgians 1714–1837

Leatherhead in Georgian times was a thriving community concentrating mainly on agriculture. There were landowners with large estates offering employment to many, traders catering for the town's needs and a regular coach and postal connection with the neighbouring towns and London.

## The town and its population

A large-scale map of Leatherhead drawn up by George Gwilt in 1782/3 shows the layout of the streets was basically the same as it was before the new town centre was built in 1982, 200 years later. Only the stretch of the turnpike road from the east end of the town to the church has long since disappeared into Church Road. The main change was in the naming of the streets. Great Queen Street became the High Street and Little Queen Street became Church Street. Kingston Road was once Bradmere Lane and Randalls Road, Patsoms Lane. Unfenced tracks crossed the large open Common Field, whose boundary was near the church and Worple Road. 'Worple' means 'trackway'. There was more common land near Sweech House where Fairfield Road is now and it seems probable that the annual Leatherhead Fair was held there each October. The population at this period was less than 1,000 but by the taking of the first national census in 1801 it had increased to 1,078 and, in 1831, to 1,724.

## Principal families

It is surprising that very few families prominent in Stuart times in Leatherhead remained so in the Georgian period. The Gardiners, Sands, Rogers, Skeetes, Akehursts and Godmans disappeared and only the Daltons, the last of the major 17th-century families, survived. Even they died out in the middle of this century. The Dacres, connected through marriage to the Godmans, continued to occupy Church House until the mid-1740s.

Among the new families, one of the most important were the Gores, who took over The Mansion from the Akehursts during the third decade of the century. Although the house was said to have been rebuilt in 1710, Lt. General Humphrey Gore, governor of Kinsale and a colonel in the King's Own Dragoons, made further alterations to it. After his death in 1739 the property passed to his son Henry and then, in 1777, to Henry's daughter Catherine, wife of William Wade who became the sole owner when she died in 1786.

William Wade was a noted figure at Court. He was Master of Ceremonies at Bath and Brighton in 1769 and shared with his master, the Prince Regent, a good-humoured liveliness and a love of gaming and of clothes. In fact, he thought of himself as something of a style-setter in opposition to Beau Brummell, as his portrait by Gainsborough shows. He held his post at Brighton until 1808, dying there two years later. William Wade owned not only The Mansion but also Church House. Tragically, his only son, Gore Wade, his wife, grandson and three infant children were all lost at sea in 1813 on an East Indiaman, the *John Palmer.*

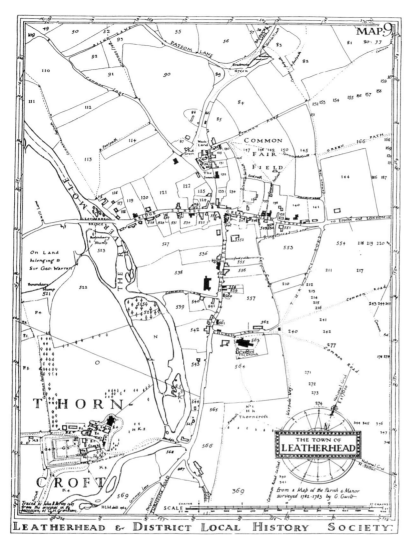

**36** Map of Leatherhead town by George Gwilt, the county surveyor in 1782.

The lord of the manor was Henry Boulton, who lived at Thorncroft Manor and Givons Grove after the last of the Daltons had died in the 1750s. Henry Crabb Boulton was Member of Parliament for Worcester. A few years after he took over Thorncroft, it was rebuilt by Sir Robert Taylor, the architect and designer of the Bank of England. The new building in the classical style was substantially the same as it is today. Boulton also commissioned 'Capability' Brown to reshape the grounds and the shell bridge was presumably designed by him. He cut a canal in the river to create Thorncroft Island. When his nephew, another Henry, took over the lease of the property, the family also owned the manors of Pachenesham and Headley. It was Henry who commissioned George Gwilt to produce the large-scale maps of Leatherhead.

Lord Carpenter bought Randalls Park in 1753. His son, created Earl of Tyrconnel in 1761, sold the property 30 years later. It had belonged to the Sands family in Tudor times and for the whole of the last century. There

**37** A glimpse of Church House in 1822 from a water-colour by J. Hassell.

**38** William Wade in a portrait by Gainsborough. He was Master of the Revels for the Prince Regent at Brighton and Bath and lived in The Mansion.

**39**   Thorncroft Manor as it is today.

**40**   The Shell Bridge, thought to have been designed by 'Capability' Brown, at Thorncroft.

## THE POOR MURDERED WOMAN.

1.
It was Hankey the squier, as I have heard say,
Who rode out a-hunting on one Saturday.
They hunted all day, but nothing they found
But a poor murdered woman, laid on the cold ground.

2.
About eight o'clock, boys, our dogs they throwed off,
On Leatherhead Common, and that was the spot;
They tried all the bushes, but nothing they found
But a poor murdered woman, laid on the cold ground.

3.
They whipped their dogs off, and kept them away,
For I do think it's proper he should have fair play;
They tried all the bushes, but nothing they found
But a poor murdered woman, laid on the cold ground.

4.
They mounted their horses, and rode off the ground,
They rode to the village, and alarmed it all round;
" It is late in the evening, I am sorry to say,
She can not be removed until the next day."

5.
The next Sunday morning, about eight o'clock,
Some hundreds of people to the spot they did flock;
For to see the poor creature your heart would have bled,
Some odious violence had come to her head.

6.
She was took off the common, and down to some inn,
And the man that has kept it, his name is John Simm.
The coroner was sent for, the jury they joined,
And soon they concluded, and settled their mind.

7.
Her coffin was brought; in it she was laid,
And took to the churchyard that was called Leatherhead;
No father, no mother, nor no friend, I'm told,
Come to see that poor creature put under the mould.

8.
So now I'll conclude, and finish my song,
And those that have done it, they will find themselves wrong.
For the last day of Judgment the trumpet will sound,
And their souls not in heaven, I'm afraid, won't be found.

*(Sung by Mr. Foster, 1897.)*

**41**   The ballad of *The Poor Murdered Woman* written in 1834 refers to an actual local murder.

**42**   Watercolour of Randalls Park House by John Hassell in 1822.

were several ownership changes after the Carpenters gave it up, Sir John Coghill acquiring it in 1802 and Nathaniel Bland in 1810. In 1839 the old house was demolished and a new one built, not necessarily on the original site.

The Rogers family who had occupied the Rectory on the site of the present Vale Lodge no longer appeared in Leatherhead's records. The Rectory House may have fallen into disrepair, as Vale Lodge was built on the site.

A famous naval officer lived in Linden House, now the site of a similarly named block of flats in Epsom Road. Richard Byron was the brother of Admiral John Byron, known in naval circles as 'Foulweather Jack', who was grandfather of the poet. Rear Admiral Richard Byron himself had a distinguished career and commanded the *Belvedere* against the *United States of America* in the American War of Independence.

## Some of the town's artistic connections

Jane Austen often visited Bookham where her mother's first cousin lived, the wife of the vicar Samuel Cooke. It has been suggested that Highbury, in her novel *Emma,* is actually a portrait of Leatherhead. The fact that Randalls existed here as a house, and in 1761 a Mr. Knightly was actually a church benefactor, helps to substantiate the theory.

Many writers came to the area. Apart from Matthew Arnold living at Cobham, Richard Brinsley Sheridan at Polesden Lacey and, in the town, John O'Keefe, George Meredith lived at Flint Cottage on Box Hill. Keats, it is claimed, finished his poem *Endymion* while staying at the *Fox and Hounds*, now the *Burford Bridge Hotel*.

Although not actually resident in the town, artists came to Leatherhead to sketch and paint the surrounding countryside. Cotman, Peter de Wint, Girtin and J.M.W. Turner were among the many young artists encouraged by Dr.

**43**   Watercolour of Leatherhead parish church.

Monro both at his Adelphi residence and his country home in Bell Lane, Fetcham. Turner said they were given 'half a crown for their sketch and a good supper'. He considered Dr. Monro his first patron. Dr. Monro and his father were both leading physicians at the Bethlehem Hospital, known as Bedlam, where they studied and treated mental illness. Indeed, it was Dr. Monro who certified Turner's mother as insane and committed her to his hospital.

Gerard van der Gucht, one of 40 children born to the engraver of the same name, was a Leatherhead resident according to his marriage entry in the Richmond parish register in 1759. His brother, Benjamin, was one of the original students at the Royal Academy in 1768. He became a portrait painter and the proprietor of a picture gallery and was accidentally drowned at Chiswick in 1794.

## Farming

This was a century of great agricultural improvement, with the growth of root crops and the introduction of new equipment which, together with better rotations, helped to revolutionise crop and livestock production. Some of the new ideas, such as the use of clover and lucerne as fodder crops, had been adopted by Leatherhead farms in the late 17th century. There was a four-year crop rotation: turnips followed by barley, then clover and finally wheat. Most farms kept livestock, sheep and hogs predominating, and cattle for meat and dairy purposes. Wiltshire and Dorset sheep as well as pure South Down sheep were mainly bred.

Compared with levels in Stuart times, crop production and dairy output increased in the area during the Georgian period, but no records of how successful the farmers were have survived. There were harvest fluctuations; thus 1740 was a 'dearth' year and, although good years followed, there were bad harvests again in 1756 and 1757 when the price of food rose and riots broke out in some parts of the country.

Leatherhead still farmed traditionally. The town still had the large open arable Common Field and common pasture grounds whose use was watched over by the manorial courts. Pasturing of sheep on the land before the crops had been harvested, and on the meadows before the completion of the hay harvest, were still common offences, as was the encroaching or enclosing of pieces of land.

When drawing up land leases, it was customary to ensure that the new occupier farmed the land well. Only two cereal crops were to be grown in successive years on the same field, trees were not to be felled and fences, hedges and ditches had to be maintained. Such concern can be understood since most of the walnut trees so greatly admired by John Evelyn in Norbury Park were felled. Sold to the government to become British Army rifle stocks, they were mainly used in the fight against the colonists in the American War of Independence.

## Farms

There were 10 farms outside the area of the Common Field in the Leatherhead area during the 18th century, Thorncroft Manor Farm, Randalls Farm, later in Georgian times known as Holme Farm, Givons (Gibbons) Grove Farm, Bocketts Farm, Highlands Farm, adjoining Leatherhead Common Field, Barnett Wood Farm, New Pond Farm, north of Leatherhead Common, Rowhurst Farm, near New Pond Farm, Vale Lodge Farm, the successor to the farm on the Rectory, and Sweech Farm at 2 Gravel Hill.

## Roads and road traffic

Turnpikes from Leatherhead to Epsom, Dorking, Horsham and Guildford were constructed in 1755 and 1758 and the maintenance of the turnpikes was paid for by a system of tolls. The toll-house was in Great Queen Street (High Street) near the present Leatherhead Institute. There was some urgency for the roads to be improved since the Seven

**44**   Highlands Farm as it is today.

**45**   John Rocque's map of 1770 showing the road patterns.

Years' War with France broke out in 1756, increasing the need for assured movement of men and materials to the south coast. Hay, straw and oats were stored in magazines in Dorking's chalk and sandstone caves and in Leatherhead between the toll-house and the church, close to the present Magazine Place. Church Road was at one time called Magazine Lane. Two regiments of Surrey militia were formed at this time and in 1779 recruits for the forces were said to be 'coming in daily' to Leatherhead to join those stationed there.

The pattern of roads in the Leatherhead area at this period is shown on John Rocque's map of 1770. Apart from the main roads to Ashtead and Epsom, Cobham, Guildford and Dorking, there are a number of roads connecting them on the map with tracks across the Leatherhead Common Field and the Downs near Mickleham.

Because of its importance to traffic, the upkeep of Leatherhead bridge over the Mole was a continuing problem for the parish officers, as it had been in the past centuries. Early in the 18th century, the bridge was described as 'a fine stone bridge' and as a 'stately fabric of stones and piles laid upon one another'. In the Vestry Minutes of 1695-1739 there are several references to the three and a half acres near the bridge, the revenue from which was used for the bridge's maintenance. As much as £4 3s. 4d. was allotted for repair in 1724. Because of the constant need of repair, the bridge was at this time barred off and reserved only for those paying towards its upkeep and they were issued with their own keys. Most other travellers used the ford alongside. In 1774 the Surrey justices considered that, although parts of the bridge were well preserved, other parts were a danger to the public and they recommended that the bridge should be repaired and enlarged. The parish was much relieved when in 1782, by an Act of Parliament, Leatherhead bridge and bridges elsewhere in Surrey, were made the responsibility of the county authorities.

George Gwilt, the county surveyor and mapmaker, rebuilt the bridge in 1782/3, widening it with small safety refuges for pedestrians and using Portland stone cramped with wrought iron for the parapets. Old bricks from Ashtead Park were used above the arches. This is the bridge as seen today. The present lamp standards were added during recent refurbishment by Surrey County Council.

**46**    The Leatherhead bridge from a painting by J. Varley.

**47** Leatherhead bridge as seen today.

## Grand Imperial Ship Canal

This was the brainchild of the architect and engineer Nicholas Wilcox Cundy in 1825. He planned a canal 150ft. wide and 28ft. deep, able to accommodate the largest ships afloat. It was to run 78 miles from Rotherhithe to Spithead passing through Wandsworth, Malden and Epsom Common to Leatherhead Bridge and on to Mickleham, Dorking and Arundel. Huge locks would raise the canal 127ft. between Ewell and Epsom to the 21-mile long summit level.

The Rennie Brothers surveyed and reported that this route would be feasible. They estimated the cost at £6½ million, an enormous sum at that time. Others thought it would never yield an adequate return. So the great scheme died, never again to be seriously revived.

## Coach services

Frequent horse-drawn coach services passed through Leatherhead to and from London and neighbouring towns, continuing what was started in Stuart times. Later in the century there was a regular service leaving Epsom, Croydon, Dorking, Guildford and Horsham. With the exception of Sunday, the Brighton coach left Leatherhead at 2 p.m. and the post, arriving at 3 p.m. daily, left by mail coach for London at 10 p.m. nightly. By 1838 there were daily coaches to Arundel, Bognor and Worthing. Driving a coach could be hazardous and there was often an armed guard alongside the driver. In July 1827 *The Times* reported the waylaying of a mail wagon as it travelled from Dorking to Kingston, just opposite Givons Grove, the home of Captain Boulton. There was a cry of 'The money or your life' and the driver, although seriously injured by bullets, attempted to return fire and drive on. The sound of gunfire brought Captain Boulton and his gamekeeper to the rescue. The mail got through but the assailants escaped and the GPO offered 100 guineas reward for information leading to a conviction.

Most stage-coaches stopped at the *Swan Hotel*, described in 1791 as 'a very genteel house with good accommodation, most excellent stabling and good post chaises with able horses for hire'. Trout from the River Mole was one of the specialities served and Pepys recorded earlier having sampled the dish. There was another stage-coach stop at the *Duke's Head* at the top of Great Queen Street.

**48** Advertisement for the *Swan* inn.

## A royal accident

On 8 October 1806 there was an accident on the bend outside the *Swan*. A coach carrying Princess Caroline, the wife of the Prince Regent, to visit her friends, the Locks of Norbury Park, overturned while rounding the corner at speed. The Princess and her ladies were thrown out on to the road and one, Miss Harriet Cholmondeley, was killed instantly. A memorial to her was erected in the parish church.

## Church and parish

For the whole of the first half of the 18th century there was only one vicar of Leatherhead, Robert Johnson. He had taken the living as a young man in 1689 and held it for 63 years. Robert Laxton, a Fellow of St John's College, Cambridge, was the next incumbent in 1752; he improved the Vicarage, was a 'worthy vicar' and was killed by a fall from his horse. It was after Robert Laxton's death in 1767 that the parish had to be satisfied for many years with curates taking the services. The new vicar, Samuel Markham, held the living for 30 years but was often an absentee. It seems he preferred to live in London where he was the evening preacher at the church of St Dunstan-in-the-West.

There were as many as 17 curates appointed to the parish between 1771 and 1779. None of these stayed long, perhaps because of the accumulated amount of work due to the frequent absence of the vicar. Absenteeism among the clergy in the 18th century was not uncommon and so was pluralism. At the end of the century, when Richard Harvey took over from Samuel Markham as vicar in 1797 he also held the benefice of Warnham. He was appointed to this by George III and approved by the Archbishop of Canterbury. This state of affairs continued even after 1804 when the distinguished antiquarian James Dallaway became vicar, although he did choose to live and officiate in Leatherhead.

## James Dallaway

James Dallaway was born in 1763 in Bristol, the son of a banker. He was educated at Cirencester Grammar School and Trinity

**49**   Portrait of James Dallaway, distinguished antiquarian and vicar of Leatherhead from 1804 to his death in 1834.

College, Oxford, marrying Harriet Ann Jeffreys in 1780. While a young curate in Gloucestershire, he edited the memoirs of Ralph Bigland, Garter King of Arms, and as a result was elected Fellow of the Society of Antiquaries in 1789. In 1793 he published *Inquiries into the Origin and Progress of Heraldry in England*. He took a BMed degree at Oxford in 1794 and was appointed chaplain and physician to the British Embassy in Constantinople for two years. He published a history of Constantinople in 1797 and edited the works of Lady Mary Wortley Montagu, whose husband was ambassador to the Sultan in 1716. In 1797 Dallaway was appointed secretary to the Earl Marshal of England, his friend and patron the Duke of Norfolk. In 1799 the Duke gave him the living of South Stoke near Arundel which he resigned in 1803. He took over the vicarage of Slinfold as well as the rectory of Llanmaes in

Glamorganshire. It was this post that he exchanged with Richard Harvey for the vicarage of Leatherhead which he held with Slinfold for 30 years until his death. In 1811 he became a prebendary of Chichester. He is largely remembered for his academic work on Sir William Burrell's manuscript histories of Chichester and Arundel published in 1815 and 1819, although as an art historian he published other works.

It is presumed that, as secretary to the Earl Marshal, the burden of organising the extremely colourful, elaborate and expensive coronation of George IV fell on Dallaway in 1821. This was quite a contrast to the quiet backwater of Leatherhead where, as vicar with his vestry, he erected a House of Industry, the workhouse, in the north of the parish whence free medical attention was given to the sick.

Between 1820 and 1826 he initiated extensive repairs to the church, particularly to the chancel, placing the altar at the east end with new communion rails, and the east window, in which he incorporated antique stained glass he had collected in Rouen. He embodied Chi-Rho, an early Christian emblem, in the altar piece he erected and presented a silver chalice hallmarked 1661 to the church. The west door was widened for the parish fire engine to be parked there.

## First printed history of Leatherhead

In 1821 Dallaway wrote the text for 13 etchings by his wife who was a gifted artist. These featured Leatherhead, its Vicarage, church, the *Running Horse* inn and much of the surrounding countryside. Thus it was that the first separate history of the town was written and privately published by Dallaway. He died in 1834 and at his own wish was buried with his friend, author Robert Duppa, in the churchyard. The main annual lecture given by the Leatherhead and District Local History Society bears his name.

## The Vestry's care for the poor and needy

The vestry still watched over Leatherhead's welfare, with its surveyors of highways (waywardens) to care for the roads and foot-paths and its overseers for the workhouse. The vicar or curate presided over two church-wardens, four overseers and other parishioners. At their meetings the local almshouse, the work-house and caring for those in need were all dealt with.

Held in the church, the procedure of the meetings differed little from late Tudor times, all aspects of parish life being carefully logged. The overseers of the poor were chosen by the ratepayers once a year and had to be ratified by the Justice of the Peace in Epsom. The over-seers were usually tradesmen, though early in the 19th century gentlemen began to take on this responsibility. The trade interests of many of the overseers may have aroused suspicion since 4s. 6d. per person was given in 1829 to those who contracted to supply the poor with food, drink and clothing. The relief of the poor

**50**   Dallaway's church in 1808.

In 1722 the widow of Francis Hailer was provided with the following by the vestry:

| | |
|---|---|
| One feather bedd and boulster, 2 pillows, 3 blankets, 1 pare of sheets, curtains, vallens and steddle | £1 10s. 0d. |
| One warming pan | 4. 0 |
| 3 porringers | 1. 6 |
| 3 chairs | 1. 3 |
| One pare of small andirons | 1. 6 |
| One skillett | 2. 0 |
| One spitt | 10 |
| One pare of tongs | |
| One pare of pothooks | 1. 6 |
| 1 frying pan | 1. 6 |
| 1 porridge pott | 5. 0 |
| 1 table | 1. 0 |
| 1 basket and a pare of bellows | 6 |
| 1 spinning wheel | 1. 0 |
| 6 trenchers and a wooden bottle | 1. 0 |
| 1 drinking tubb, 3 crockes, 2 wooden rowles and a tundish | 1. 0 |
| 1 joynsted chest | 2. 0 |
| One round table | 1. 6 |
| One candlestick | 4 |
| | £2 17s. 11d. |

**51**  Widow Hailer's vestry provisions.

was dispensed by the churchwardens, who also collected the poor rate based on the rateable value of property in the town. In 1793 it was 9d. in the pound.

The poor were given fuel, clothes and shoes as well as loaves, this being a national custom. However, bread came with conditions and in 1752 the vestry ordered that 'those given bread on Sunday must attend church service'. Among those frequently helped were pregnant or 'big-bellied' women who seemed to be passing through on foot. Others, for example '17 sailors and 16 slaves that came out of Turkey', were given 3s. 6d. in 1723. In order to distinguish the vagrants from the parish poor, the vestry ordered in 1751 that the latter wear a badge. The able-bodied who could work were frequently housed with property holders who were paid to take them as workers. Thus, in 1747 Richard Bushel was given 1s. a week to clothe and keep Richard Martin in service for four years; for 40s. his wife undertook to look after Sarah Hail for the same number of years, provided she learnt how to milk. Idleness was frowned on by the vestry and records show that those suspected of it were often threatened with a spell in the House of Correction.

Poor children were farmed out, although it was a declining practice because of the conditions often endured by the children. Orphaned children, until they were old enough to go into service or be apprenticed, were cared for by widows. For this the widows received an average of 2s. a week. Children born out of wedlock and their mother had by law to be supported by the father. Apprenticeship was as common as it had been in the 17th century.

In 1795 a Watford silk-mill owner named Watson sought Leatherhead's poor children to work in his mills for 1s. 6d. a week in return for clothing and feeding them. It is not known what came of this offer which appeared generous although no mention is made of how many hours the children would work.

**Care of the sick**

The vestry members were concerned with the sick as well as the poor, but whereas in the 17th century they turned for help mainly to the townfolk, in the Georgian period they sought professional aid. A surgeon-apothecary lived in Leatherhead and died here in 1726. In 1784 Christopher Vine was receiving 7 guineas a year as the parish surgeon, and in 1796 Daniel Wilson, described as a surgeon, apothecary and man-midwife, received 10 guineas a year.

The parish also gave money to the sick and to those who nursed them. In 1740 Richard Tyrrell received 5s. when he was ill and Elizabeth Arrow 6s. for the month she was sick. Widows, dubbed in the records as 'Goody', were often employed as nurses.

Concern was expressed over the possible spread of smallpox in the town and in 1799, after Dr. Edward Jenner discovered the vaccine, all the poor were inoculated against it. This humanitarian measure may have had an ulterior motive but it is still a good illustration of the sensible use of parish resources to benefit the whole community. Medical treatment for other diseases was also paid for by the parish, even if this meant that patients had to travel outside its limits.

The parish was also responsible for the burial of its poor and a local tradition grew up that the carrying of a corpse for burial established a right of way. Consequently the *Swan Hotel* charged a penny for permission to bear a body through its yard.

The Leatherhead almshouse was described in 1725 as having six rooms, so it was a fairly substantial building. According to the Vestry Minutes of 1750, an inspection committee was appointed to report on the state of the building and whether or not additions should be made to it. In 1807 it was sold for the large sum of £440 and replaced by a House of Industry, a workhouse built on the common north of the town and set in two acres of land with a large garden, all donated by Henry Boulton of Thorncroft Manor.

At a national level, there were fears that the poor in the workhouses would be huddled together promiscuously. The Leatherhead vestry prevented this by paying £160 for a brick wall to be built, dividing the sleeping rooms of the men and women so that, with the exception of meal times, they would be apart both day and night. One sad result of this was that married couples and families were separated.

## Charities

While the regular financing of the poor in Leatherhead came from the poor rate, there were also several charitable bequests, including some for education purposes.

The Skeete, Smith and Hudson charities set up in the Stuart period still benefited the town. These were supplemented during the course of the 18th century by Robert Nettlefold in 1755, who left just over £20 to be distributed to the poor, and by Elizabeth Rolfe in 1777 who bequeathed the interest on £400 annually to be given to 10 of the town's poorest families in memory of Dame Catherine Thompson, buried in the churchyard. William Denne, a banker, also gave money in 1786 for the purchase of fuel for the poor and Richard Toy, tenant of the *Swan Hotel*, left the interest from £1,200 of gilt-edged securities in 1812 to be paid monthly to six old and poor parishioners. In 1834 Louisa Mary Dickins of Vale Lodge left £1,000 for the poor.

## Education and charities

The schooling of Leatherhead's children by charitable funding was a new feature. In his will of 1725, David White, a bricklayer of Ewell, provided for the poor children of Epsom, Ewell, Ashtead, Leatherhead and Abbots Langley in Hertfordshire, all parishes with which he had been associated. As far as Leatherhead was concerned, he directed that freehold property to the value of £10 a year should be purchased and the income benefit the town's children. It was paid to the vicar and churchwardens for the instruction of poor children in reading, writing, arithmetic and religion. Another charity was set up in 1796 by John Lucas, a Leatherhead wheelwright, who left the interest on £400 stock which eventually helped to pay the local schoolmaster's salary of £15 per annum and educate eight poor boys between the ages of 8 and 12. Free schools for the poor were established in the south by far-seeing London merchants anxious to ensure that, by education, Protestantism remained the established religion of the country. In so doing, they laid the foundations for grammar schools in later centuries.

There had been a free school in Leatherhead since 1596, although it is shrouded in mystery and may for a time have disappeared. Nevertheless it was there in 1832 and, according to Pigot's *Directory*, educating 10 boys.

**52** John Wesley, who preached his last sermon in Kingston House in February 1791.

Earlier, in 1712, the school had been extended to include 11 girls on subscription of £22 per annum. It is remarkable that poor girls should have been educated at such an early date, let alone outnumber the boys. However, by 1818 a day school had been set up for boys alone, the girls' section having failed. This was helped with funds from the White and Lucas charities and Joseph Green was the master. The vicar, James Dallaway, ran a Sunday school for 80 boys and 70 girls on voluntary subscriptions. The curriculum taught was the three 'R's' plus another 'R' for religion. It seems possible that the schoolroom was originally in the west tower of the church.

The first private school listed in 1791 and 1798 in the *Universal Directory* was an Academy for Young Gentlemen set up by Thomas Hopkins. Later, in 1838, there was an Academy for Boys under Thomas Hill, who was

also the Registrar of Births and Deaths. Meanwhile, in 1799 in St George's Fields, Southwark, a school for the blind was founded by four philanthropists, Thomas Boddington, Samuel Bosanquet, James Ware and William Houlston. Up to then it had been thought impossible to educate the blind, but as earlier attempts to train them for manual work had proved successful, the school was established. By 1832 it had 150 resident pupils and by 1901 it moved to a site in Leatherhead.

## Wesley's visit

Perhaps the most memorable event in Leatherhead in the late 18th century was the visit of John Wesley on 23 February 1791. He was 87 years old at the time and died a week later. During the visit he gave what was to be his last homily in an upstairs room in Kingston House. This was the last of 42,400 sermons he delivered in his ministry and he chose as his text Isaiah I v.6. He stayed the night with the father of Leatherhead's curate, Mr. Durnford, and travelled to London the following day. A legend grew up that Wesley had given his sermon beneath a cedar tree outside Kingston House. There is no evidence for this although he may have given a blessing to the assembled crowd there when the cedar can have been little more than a sapling.

## Revolution and social change

When John Wesley came to Leatherhead the French Revolution was already two years old. It had received qualified approval at first for, with the passing of the Bill for the Abolition of Slavery in 1791 and the publication of Thomas Paine's *Rights of Man*, a national social conscience seemed to be emerging. But when the Revolution's excesses culminated in the execution of Louis XVI, approval quickly turned to disapproval and fear. There was alarm when a number of assassination attempts were made on King George III, the last in 1800 when two shots fired at the Royal Box in Drury Lane Theatre narrowly missed him.

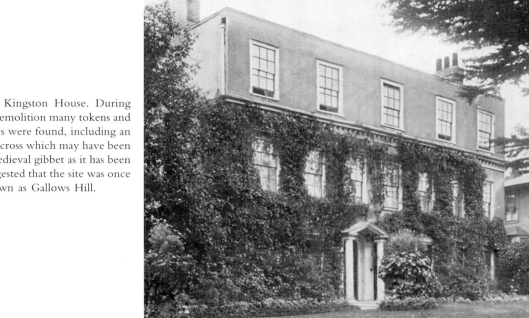

**53** Kingston House. During its demolition many tokens and coins were found, including an oak cross which may have been a medieval gibbet as it has been suggested that the site was once known as Gallows Hill.

In 1793 Britain joined the European Coalition already at war with France, so was herself at war. After Nelson's victory over the French fleet at the Battle of the Nile in 1798, there was an uneasy peace. War with France broke out again in 1803 and, as Napoleon massed his armies at Boulogne, invasion was a real threat. The whole country was roused by the danger and parishes like Leatherhead were assessed on how many able-bodied men could be mustered for the forces. Fines were imposed for failing to meet the quota. Once more Nelson was needed and there is a strong local tradition that he spent part of his last night in England here, before the decisive Battle of Trafalgar in 1805. His house at Merton was only one and a half hours from Leatherhead and it is probable he halted at the *Fox and Hounds*, now the *Burford Bridge Hotel*, to change and water his horses and feed his cavalry escort. Then moving on through Guildford and Liphook, where he drank tea by candlelight at the *Anchor*, he joined the *Victory* at Portsmouth.

Despite wars and bad harvests that caused unrest, particularly in 1830, this period of British history differs from the 17th century because of its essential unity in politics, thought and social development. The foundations of an industrialised society were being laid as the obligations of an agrarian one were beginning to break down. Judging by the 1841 census, Leatherhead itself was slowly becoming part of an urban society for among its normal trades were added watchmakers, milliners, army personnel, chemists, an excise officer and a policeman.

## Chapter Six

# The Victorian Era 1837–1901

Some 16 years before Victoria became Queen, James Dallaway, the then vicar of Leatherhead, observed that the town was rapidly converting itself by a 'multiplication of inconsiderable houses into an appendage of the enormous London', in other words, a suburb. Leatherhead had long been a favourite place for wealthy Londoners to live and their numbers greatly increased in the 19th century. Large new houses were built like Tyrrells Wood, Givons Grove, Cherkley Court and Woodlands Park. The town's central position in Surrey, on the coaching route from London to Worthing and Brighton and astride the Croydon to Guildford road, contributed to its prosperity, helped by the arrival of the railway in 1859 which made access to London so much easier. Improved facilities bettered everyone's lot, gas being supplied in 1850 and piped water in 1884, but the installation of electricity, except for the privileged few with private generators, had to wait until Edwardian times.

Despite better communications with the outside world, Leatherhead remained during these years essentially a self-contained little country town. There was a feeling of belonging to a small community where both the rich and the not-so-rich joined together in many activities. Class distinction there was, but this did not divide the people in their yearly round of sports and pastimes, concerts and celebrations. The church took the lead in supporting many ways of drawing people together. Hardly less important were the wealthy benefactors like Abraham Dixon of Cherkley Court, who founded and built the Leatherhead Institute in 1892, where for two pence a week educational and recreational activities were provided for all. The owners of large houses, like Vale Lodge and The Red House, opened their gardens for exhibitions, promenade concerts and dancing on lawns described as 'green as billiard tables'.

In 1894 a new era opened with the formation of the Urban District Council, following the establishment of the Surrey County Council six years earlier. The population doubled in size in the 40 years between 1841 and 1881 and increased by a further thousand in the last two decades of Victoria's reign to 4,694. A larger population meant that more houses were needed and developers were taking up land wherever possible.

## Local occupations and trades

Most people's work was related directly or indirectly to the land, though how they were employed changed markedly between 1841 and 1881. Those described in the census as 'agricultural labourers' had decreased appreciably, and some in 1881 referred to themselves as 'gardeners', a much larger category then than in the earlier census.

Apart from 'servants', the largest category, and those in farming, the census returns listed about sixty different occupations in Leatherhead, including building, brick-making, saw-milling and leather traders. Tanning was chiefly in the hands of the Chitty family from as early as 1826. Their works were close to Leatherhead bridge but the tannery fell on hard times in the

**54**  Leatherhead Institute, built and endowed by Abraham Dixon for the use of the town in 1892. At its official opening in 1893, the church's bellringers rang 1,893 changes.

1870s and stopped work. In 1888 one barn of the mill was opened as a swimming bath, taken over in 1900 by St John's School. After the Second World War the area was cleared to make way for Minchin Close.

Boot and shoe-making diminished in the town in the later years although most travel was still on foot or by horse. One bootmaker, Jeremiah Johns, was to be Leatherhead's first inventor since he patented a braking system for railway and other carriages, yet it was never

marketed. Saddle and harness-making flourished in Bridge Street for some 200 years, first with the Ragges and then in the 19th century, through marriage, with the Lloyds. They lived in an old timber-framed house near the top of the street, demolished in a civil defence exercise in 1939/40.

Coach-building was run by two families, the Venthams and the Karns. Charles Ventham established his works in Bridge Street in 1835. Most of his commissions were for the supply

**55** The old mill at Leatherhead bridge was once a tannery but, with its closure in 1888, one barn was opened as a swimming bath to be taken over by St John's School in 1900.

# JOHN LLOYD,
## Saddler & Harness Maker,
### LETHERHEAD & GREAT BOOKHAM.

*Carriage, Gig and other Harness warranted of the best Material & Workmanship.*

Established in the above building for 200 Years.

**56** John Lloyd inherited this saddle and harness business from his father who, by marriage, was descended from the Ragges. Emily Walker (née Lloyd) closed the business in 1905 and moved to other premises in Bridge Street selling leather goods until the 1930s. She died aged 93 in 1951. There is a branch of the family (the Tims) still living in the area.

of private carriages. In 1901 the firm moved into the era of horseless carriages. Ventham's last two coaches remained in their showrooms until 1929 when one was broken up and the other was bought by Bertram Mills for use in his circus. Daimler and Siddeley commissioned Venthams to build coach-work for their motor chassis and about 1909 the company applied to become official RAC repairers. The second coaching business, owned by the Karn family, built their carriages in the Fairfield area and also made wagons and carts and did blacksmith's work in Kingston Road.

Brewing and malting was one of the town's leading industries. The Swan Brewery was established by William Moore of the *Swan Hotel* in 1859 at what is now the entrance to the Swan Centre. A new steam brewery constructed on the tower principle was set up in 1874. Pale ale was the chief product, but stout and porter were

**57**   Bridge Street at the turn of the 20th century, showing the leather shop on the left.

**58 & 59** Two of the last carriages made by Venthams of Bridge Street.

also brewed. The water was obtained from an artesian well 200 feet deep, and in 1857 the beer was described as 'very yeasty and new'. The business continued until 1921. Another brewery in North Street was run by the Start family, who owned the *Bull* and the *Duke's Head* in 1854 as well as having an earlier interest in the *King's Head*. In 1872 it was sold to Young's of Dorking, and by 1892 had ceased brewing and only malting continued.

Early records mentioned many beer-houses and beer-sellers. In 1841 there was a beer-house at the top of Gravel Hill run by Joseph Green, who by 1851 was described as 'beer-seller and schoolmaster'. In another 10 years, the upwardly mobile Mr. Green is described as a 'proprietor of houses'. The *Jug House*, now 1 Church Walk, sold beer and maybe cider, obviously by the jug.

Late in the century, Duke and Ockenden with premises at Hampton Cottage in Church Street were the largest manufacturers of drilling rigs for water supply in the country, producing the Norton Tube Well for well-drilling in difficult soils.

There were, of course, many shops open until a late hour, especially on Saturdays when wages were paid. The High Street was busy with carriages whose coachmen tapped on shop windows with their whips, and wares were brought out for the customers in the carriages to make a choice.

## Leading families

Abraham Dixon, who came with his family to Leatherhead in 1871, was a wealthy Midlands industrialist who was about to retire. Almost every good cause, whether for the church or for the town, benefited from Abraham's generosity. He gave a substantial sum for the building of All Saints' church in 1888 and for the restoration of the parish church three years later. However, his major contribution was the building of the Institute in 1892. The opening ceremony was in 1893 and the church bellringers rang 1,893 changes for the occasion. The Institute flourished, with wide-ranging activities from billiards to pigeon clubs, concerts and whist drives. When Abraham Dixon died in 1907, two of his daughters continued teaching art and cookery there.

**60** Drawing by A.J. Ginger showing the side of Lloyd's saddlers shop leading to a rope walk where ropes for harnesses were made and stored.

**61** The Swan Brewery. Taken from a drawing for a 1920s advertisement and lent by Mary Rice-Oxley, who was told it had been used as a backing for a cupboard!

**62** A terracotta panel of flowers rescued from the Swan Brewery now incorporated into No. 31 High Street.

**63** Hartshorn butchers in North Street, 1890, had their own slaughterhouse, which distressed the children attending school behind the Congregational chapel on the right.

**64** North Street in 1905 when the school was eventually shut.

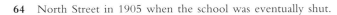

**65** The High Street with the *King's Head* at the top of the street, 1905.

**66** Abraham Dixon, a great local benefactor.

Givons Grove was owned by the Boulton family during the first half of the 19th century, but a Baring Brothers banker, Russell Sturgis, later acquired the estate and the whole property stayed with the Sturgis family until 1919 when it was sold to Humphrey Verdon Roe, the aircraft manufacturer and husband of Marie Stopes.

When Roger Cunliffe first came to the district in the 1860s he lived at Fetcham Lodge, and he stayed there until his Tyrrells Wood house was built to his design in about 1880. His son Walter, also a banker and from 1913 Governor of the Bank of England, lived at Headley Court and became the first Baron of Headley.

The Tates, who lived at Downside in the late 19th century, were from the sugar merchants Tate & Lyle and endowed the Tate Gallery. Alfred Tate was a gardening enthusiast, and from the verandah of his Italianate house 1,000 roses spread out upon the sloping garden and honeysuckles wound round the many arches. Mrs. Tate had a rose named after her and one of the gardeners, William Meuse, and his wife gave their name to two varieties of carnation. Alfred Tate committed suicide in 1913 after a serious throat operation.

Edward Budd came to Vale Lodge in 1861. He quickly made his mark as churchwarden, manager of the local schools and trustee of the Epsom and Leatherhead Friendly Society. The church lectern and two side windows commemorate him. The Leach family became owners of Vale Lodge after 1901.

Only Downs Lane separated Vale Lodge and Elm Bank House and their owners, the Budds and the Rickards, were friends. Rickards' son, Lionel, married Budd's daughter Isabel in 1882, so the friendship became even closer. Edward J. Rickards and his family came to Elm Bank in the 1870s. Elm Bank grounds were often open for social functions, especially those connected with the church. Edward Rickards was a churchwarden for a long time and was for 19 years chairman of the

**67** Marie Stopes in 1905 when she graduated as the youngest Doctor of Science in the country.

**68**   Thorncroft bridge leading to Elm Bank House, which was eventually demolished for the St Mary's Road estate.

**69**   An 1847 engraving showing Thorncroft Manor and Bridge Cottage. Below the bridge is a freshwater spring called the Sharnwell.

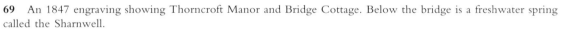

Leatherhead Parochial Committee concerned mainly with water supply and sanitation. His wife arranged for the erecting of the church's lychgate in memory of Harriet Millett in 1885.

There were as many as half a dozen lease-holders of Thorncroft Manor in the Victorian period. In 1837 Colonel John Drinkwater Bethune acquired the lease from Merton College, Oxford. He was the author of a military classic *The Siege of Gibraltar* and in 1839 his daughter published a long poem about the River Mole. The house passed to a number of tenants until the late 1890s when it was a private school in the hands of Walter Lawrence; he sublet part of the estate to Emily Moore of the *Swan Hotel*. Arthur Tritton J.P., who lived at The Priory nearby, bought the freehold from Merton College in 1904, ending Thorncroft's association with the College which had lasted over 600 years.

The Mansion, owned by Colonel W.H. Spicer in the first few years of Queen Victoria's reign, passed in 1844 to Nathaniel Bland of Randalls Park who let it to Dr. Joseph Payne for use as a private grammar school. There was a school there for about thirty years, closing in 1878. In the following year, Arthur T. Miller bought the house, which he owned until 1916.

There were other large houses close to the centre of Leatherhead, notably Windfield House owned by the Still family, Kingston House, eventually the home of Emily Moore, the proprietor of the *Swan*, Elm House, where the *New Bull Hotel* later stood, and Linden House, where a diplomat, Lord Loftus, lived. Early in the century another house on this site was occupied by Admiral Byron, brother of the poet's grandfather. The largest houses in the north of the town were Belmont Lodge (later The Red House), Randalls Park and, on the parish outskirts, Woodlands Park.

G.F. Richardson and his father before him were the early owners of Belmont Lodge standing at the top of Bull Hill. In 1873 it was bought by Henry Courage of the brewing family. He renovated Belmont Lodge and

**70**   Colonel John Drinkwater Bethune, who lived at Thorncroft.

renamed it The Red House. In 1892 the Courage family sold The Red House to Wickham Noakes, another wealthy brewer. Unlike the Noakes, Mr. and Mrs. Robert Henderson had been living at Randalls Park since 1856 when they bought it from Nathaniel Bland, who had built a new house on the site in 1829. A small chapel in the grounds, known locally as 'Pachenesham Cathedral', was thought to have been built for the use of railway navvies. Monthly services were conducted by a Leatherhead curate. The altar could be partitioned off and during the week the building became a social centre for estate staff.

In the late 1870s Woodlands Park was sold to Frederick Carkeet Bryant, a director and one of the sons of the founder of Bryant & May, the match manufacturers. He built a new modern house on the site in 1885, with several bathrooms with hot and cold running water and electric light. Woodlands Park provided kennels for the Surrey Farmers' stag hounds in the 1890s on land bordered by Oaklawn Road. Bryant, who retired in 1888, the year of the famous matchgirls' strike, died in 1897.

The story of that strike is legendary, since it resulted in the formation of the first women's trade union, the Union of Women Match-makers. Backed by Fabian reformers and a strike fund with none other than George Bernard Shaw as one of the cashiers, the women won improved wages and working conditions. It is a nice quirk of history that the musical *The Matchgirls* based on the strike story was first performed in Leatherhead's Thorndike Theatre in 1965 before transferring to the West End for a successful run.

## Farming

The quality of the farming at the beginning of the century had been criticised for neglected pastures, no manuring, low yields and poor stock. These criticisms were repeated in the early 1850s, but things slowly improved in the next 20 years.

Then, sadly, from 1870 cereal and wool prices fell throughout the country because of large US imports coinciding with many poor harvests, heavy rains and a serious outbreak of sheep-rot in 1878. Leatherhead did not suffer as much as other cereal-growing areas mainly because it was sustained by the demands for regular supplies of dairy products by the growing nearby towns.

## The farms

These were mostly held in tenancies from the large landowners like Roger Cunliffe of Tyrrells Wood and Robert Henderson of Randalls Park. In addition Thorncroft, Downside, Vale Lodge and Randalls Park all had home farms close by. Apart from these, one of the largest farms was Highlands Farm (let by Roger Cunliffe) with a farmhouse dating from about 1800, a granary

barn and a well-house, and in 1873 said to be growing wheat, barley, oats, clover and turnips. Sheep were driven along the roads from the farm to graze in rotation on the field (now Windmill estate) at the back of the Blind School and then on land behind Fetcham church on what was then a polo field, before returning to Highlands Farm the same way. Ploughing matches were also held there.

Other farms included New Pond Farm near Ashtead Common; Barnett Wood Farm, on both sides of Barnett Wood Lane, owned by Merton College, Oxford; and Bocketts Farm, south of Thorncroft. All Leatherhead farms were described in some detail by the Tithe Redemption Award dating from 1840 which has been called the 'Victorian Domesday'. The Award was welcomed since it commuted the tithes payment which had always been a contentious issue.

For many centuries Leatherhead had a large open arable field, cultivated in strips, common meadows and wastes. These were compulsorily enclosed in two Awards of 1862 and 1865, the first dealing with the common arable field and the Downs and the second with the north common lands. The Leatherhead Common Meadow was excluded from both Awards since a court case in 1849 had established the public's right to have access to the meadow. The land continues as common land right up to the present day.

## Stage-coaches and turnpikes

In the 1830s and early 1840s, as many as eight stage-coaches passed through the town every day except on Sunday. Passengers were perched on top with some seated more comfortably inside and the guard and coachmen were smartly uniformed. In the *Swan* yard the ostlers changed the steaming horses for a fresh set of four. In less than half an hour they were away again. On May Day and other festive occasions the coachman's whipstock would be decorated with ribbons and flowers, and the horses with coloured rosettes. The coaches which drove

**71**   Coach leaving the *Swan*, 1905.

through Leatherhead included the *Accommodation* coach, going to Worthing like *The Sovereign* but arriving in the town half an hour earlier. There were *The Comet*, which went to Bognor from London, *The Star*, which left London for Horsham mid-afternoon so did not reach Leatherhead until the early evening, and *The Times*, which ran to Guildford and arrived in Leatherhead late in the day.

The stage-coaches were brightly coloured in yellow, blue or black with gold trimmings. They carried four passengers inside and as many as 12 outside. They had to stop every 10 miles for a change of horses. Their average speed was about 10 m.p.h. The coaches had no proper brakes but on steep hills, an iron plate, a skidpan or drag, applied to the rear wheels acted as a primitive form of braking. One is embedded in the wall of the St Mary's Road side of Gimcrack Hill. It is a modest memorial to a carter, George Clark, who died in a wagon accident there.

All the coaches in Leatherhead were owned by the famous London proprietors, William Chaplin and B.W. Horne. The coaches started from the *Golden Cross* at Charing Cross, the *White Horse* in Fetter Lane, the *Old Bell*, Holborn, and the *Spread Eagle*, Gracechurch Street. Only the reasonably well-to-do used them since it cost as much as 5d. a mile for an inside seat, though it was cheaper and chillier to ride outside. Booking ahead was usual, half being paid at the start of the journey. The term 'booking office' is said to be a survival of the coaching age.

Coaches continued well into the 1840s and there were still eight a day in 1845, even though by this time railways were reaching out from London into Surrey and to the south coast. By the early 1850s they were replaced by horse-drawn omnibuses which met the trains at Epsom. The omnibuses for short journeys to Epsom station were drawn by three horses abreast. They were sometimes called Shillibers after the man who first introduced them to London in 1829. Horse-drawn carriers which had served Leatherhead for many years before and during the coaching age continued. Two main carriers were Thomas Bullen and William Poulter who provided a daily service to and from London.

## The arrival of the railways

Leatherhead had its first steam railway service when a line from Epsom was opened on 1 February 1859 by the London and South Western Railway (LSWR). The first station was built on the east side of the Kingston Road. The original engine house was leased out as a church and school after 1877, and still existed in 1988 but was then demolished. From July 1859 onwards, the LSWR shared the Epsom-Leatherhead line with the London, Brighton and South Coast Railway (LBSCR), and shortly after this trains from Leatherhead reached both Waterloo (LSWR) and London Bridge (LBSCR).

**72** With the coming of the railways from 1859 onwards, provision was made for travellers. This is an early watercolour of the *Railway Arms*.

**73** The original *Railway Arms* with its modern counterpart adjacent. The latter is currently being demolished.

Work began on the line to Dorking and the south coast in the mid-sixties. This new line, backed by the LBSCR, meant that trains would be continuing through Leatherhead, so the old Kingston Road station was abandoned and two new stations were built adjacent to each other nearer the town. They began operating on 11 March 1867 when the Leatherhead to Dorking line was opened. This was extended to Horsham on 1 May.

The LBSCR station remains substantially as it was then. The adjacent LSWR station, with the service road between them, continued to be a terminus until 2 February 1885 when the railway link with Guildford via Bookham and Effingham was completed. By this time, Leatherhead had railway connections not only with London but also with many parts of Surrey and the coast. When the line to Guildford was under construction, the vicar of Leatherhead invited the Navvy Mission Society to give classes and services probably at Pachenesham (now called Pachesham) to the railway workers, or navvies as they were then called.

Travelling by train was an adventure for most people in those days, and the local Leatherhead papers tempted their readers to try out many arranged excursions by train. The railway also speeded up the postal services and local farmers could market their fresh products more quickly and further afield.

**Cycling, motoring and more stage-coaches**

Roads made a come-back in the late Victorian period mainly because of the pedal cycle and the invention of the motor car. Modern bicycles first became prominent in the 1880s. A Cycling Club was formed by the Leatherhead Institute in May 1897 and in August that year cyclists were entertained at Cherkley. During the 1890s motoring was a luxury for the few, yet a police report in March 1899 complained of motor cars racing through the town on Saturday afternoons and Sundays as fast as 15-20 m.p.h. The speed limit then was about 12 m.p.h., an improvement on the 4 m.p.h. imposed by the Red Flag Act repealed in 1896.

Why should the out-dated stage-coach reappear at a time when motoring was all the rage? Nostalgia for times past attracted the wealthy, who invested in new coaches to provide a private service as a hobby for their friends and indulged themselves by being the coachmen. Regular coach services had stopped in the early 1860s. During the 1890s coaches with the splendid names of *The Old Berkeley*, *The Rocket* and *The Perseverance* changed horses in the *Swan* yard; the last two maintained a regular service in summer to Box Hill and Dorking. Another coach, *The Tally Ho*, ran from Hampton Court every weekday morning through Leatherhead to Dorking. A further reason for the rejuvenation of coaching was the Post Office's dislike of the heavy dues the railways charged on parcels, so they re-introduced the mail-coach from 1887 onwards. Leatherhead was on the route used by the new mail-coach.

## Public services

Modern water supplies were at last introduced to Leatherhead, gas revolutionised lighting and heating and notable improvements were made in the police, fire, postal and medical services. The town had long been fortunate in having water available from shallow wells, but as the population grew and land further away from the river began to be developed, deeper wells were necessary. The impetus to provide piped water in 1884 came when well water was often con-taminated. The Leatherhead and District Water Company supplied water to Leatherhead, Ashtead, Mickleham, Fetcham, the Bookhams, Stoke d'Abernon and Cobham. The main source was a 12-inch bore-hole, 200ft. deep, sited in the angle in the chalk between Waterway Road, the River Mole and Bridge Street. From the bore-hole, water flowed to a shallow well from which it was pumped to a service reservoir, now disused but still surviving, close to the top of Reigate Road. The pipes were at first only a little below ground, but after 1895 all mains were lowered to a minimum of 3ft. which is still

standard today. A new and larger reservoir was commissioned in 1897 at Highlands Farm and this still remains the service reservoir for the area. A second bore-hole was drilled in 1898 to meet increasing water demands.

Proper sanitation made slower progress than piped water. A vestry sanitary committee with good intentions tried to improve matters from 1868 onwards. Most of the outfall through sewers went into the River Mole. As a temporary measure which, however, lasted several years, the local Medical Officer of Health, Dr. Jacob, recommended in 1881 the adopting of the Rochdale Pail dry closet system and hundreds of these were ordered. The vestry committee thought them a great success and in November 1883 they even believed there was no need for any elaborate or costly sewerage scheme for Leatherhead. Eight years later they were still talking in the same vein, but in October 1893 Dr. Jacob ordered new sewers. These were not completed until January 1900.

## Gas and electricity

Gas was first delivered to Leatherhead on 3 February 1851. Now for the first time there was lighting other than candles and oil lamps, and to everyone's delight the streets were lit. The gasworks and the gasholders were north of the town on the Kingston Road near the railway bridge. In the first few years, coal supplies had to come from Deptford Wharf to Epsom by rail, then by road carrier, but after 1859, when the railway reached Leatherhead, transport problems eased. Street lighting was provided only from October to March and, even then, not on moonlit nights. Delicate incandescent mantles replaced the old-style street lamps in 1899. The Gas Company shared offices with the Water Company yet the two companies remained strictly independent.

Electricity did not come to Leatherhead universally until after the death of Queen Victoria. The stumbling block was almost always how expensive it would be for the town. Electric lighting at Cherkley Court and The

Red House was admired by all, so the large houses with their own generators led the way.

## The Police

Law and order in Leatherhead and other country parishes had for centuries been the responsibility of one or more constables selected by the manorial court from good and true local men approved by J.P.s. The spur for change came with the increasing lawlessness after the end of the Napoleonic Wars, but Sir Robert Peel's 'Bobbies' were not to be seen in Leatherhead until after 1851. Then the town had an inspector of police and one or two constables. The police station in the Fairfield had a secure room to keep offenders overnight. The early policemen wore stove-pipe hats, soon to be replaced by helmets.

## Fire services

Unlike today, Leatherhead's firemen were not full-time professionals but volunteers. The fire engine, drawn by horses who also drew the dustcart, had been kept in the church tower

**74**  The Leatherhead horse-drawn fire engine, 1905. These horses also drew the dustcart.

**75**  The fire engine house in the clock tower with the pole on which the hoses were hung to dry.

early in the century and as late as October 1846 the Vestry Minutes emphasised the need to keep it 'in an efficient state'. The clock tower was built for it close to Sweech House in the 1850s and a new engine was delivered for the 1887 Jubilee celebrations.

## Postal services

Until the 1840s letters were delivered once a day, reaching the town during the night and picked up from the Royal Mail coach at Kingston on its way to Portsmouth. By 1850 practically all the country's letters went by rail, but it was nine years before the mail came straight to the door. Rowland Hill's penny post of 1840 popularised letter-writing, and by the 1860s Leatherhead had two deliveries and two dispatches of mail a day, increasing to three in about 1880 and to four in 1899. The post office was then in Bridge Street. There was also a telegraph service at this post office, but in the last decade of the century the telephone was taking over more and more from the telegram. In May 1899 many improvements were made and a public telephone booth was installed in the High Street.

## Medical and social services

There had been doctors, or surgeons as they were sometimes called, in Leatherhead before the Victorian period. The medical services had greatly improved by the mid-19th century and there were never less than two or three doctors working in the town. A veterinary surgeon first appeared in 1851, and two were practising by the end of the century.

Dr. Jacob was the local Medical Officer of Health. In January 1887 he recommended there should be a hospital in Leatherhead for infectious diseases as the usual practice was to remove the patient to a London hospital and disinfect their house. In November 1893 a cottage hospital was opened at 8 Clinton Road in a property donated by Mrs. Sackville Davis. It took eight patients and its matron had been trained at Guy's Hospital.

The Poor Law Amendment Act of 1834, which established workhouses under a Board of Guardians centred in Epsom, took away some of the caring tasks of the vestry. Nevertheless parish charities continued their good work and vestry members strongly supported the allotment scheme for the poor after the enclosing of Leatherhead's common land in the 1860s. Twenty-five acres on either side of Barnett Wood Lane were set aside for this. There were 110 allotments altogether for which the holders paid a low monthly rental.

In the 1870s the vestry arranged for District Visitors to call on poor families and report any cases of sickness or distress. In Leatherhead, there were 15 District Visitors, mostly the wives in well-known local families like Mrs. Budd, Mrs. Rickards and Mrs. Courage and even the Headmaster of St John's School, the Rev. E.C. Hawkins. The church also sponsored a Provident Coal Club subsidised by wealthy parishioners to help those who could not afford winter coal.

In the very first *Parish Magazine* of January 1880 the vicar strongly advocated the use of the Penny Bank and the Post Office Savings Bank. Then there were the 'slate' clubs designed to encourage the savings habit, set up mainly in public houses. About this time, a Leatherhead and District Co-operative Society was founded and the general store based on their profit-sharing principle was opened in North Street. There was an almshouse for old people in Church Walk. Other social arrangements included many Friendly Societies

## The National Schools

It was not until Queen Victoria's accession that true progress was made towards giving local children the rudiments of education. The initiative locally came from the vicar of Leatherhead, the Rev. Benjamin Chapman, who founded the town's first National School in July 1838.

The Leatherhead School was in Highlands Road and it originally consisted of one

**76** All Saints' Church in 1895.

classroom to take 80 boys. In 1839 another classroom was added and this was the girls' school. Ten years later, yet another room provided an infants' school for boys and girls from three to seven years old. This gradually became more overcrowded, so in 1865 a separate school, known as the Infants' School on Gravel Hill, was built in what is now Upper Fairfield Road. This building still exists next door to the British Legion Hall. The Infants' School and the Boys' School in Highlands Road remained as schools until 1912.

Another infants' school, the future All Saints' School, opened in July 1877. The school was in the then-disused engine house off the Kingston Road which doubled as a Sunday school and a Mission church. After All Saints' church was completed in 1889 it was decided to raise funds for a new building for the Infants'

School, which by this time was known as All Saints' School. On 25 April 1900 the new school was formally opened in what in 1978 was to become the North Leatherhead Community Centre. So, after nearly a quarter of a century in the old engine shed, the school moved into its new home for another three-quarters of a century.

Many years before all this, the Boys' and Girls' Schools in Highlands Road had become overcrowded, and in 1884 a site was purchased on which to build a separate school for the girls. The building which later became Poplar Road Church of England First School was erected as the National School for Girls and opened on 10 January 1884.

There was a nonconformist school at the back of the old Congregational church in North Street known as the British School, because it was aided by the British and Foreign School Society, the nonconformist equivalent of the National Society. A critical report in 1901 by the Board of Education architect led to the closing of the school in 1902, though the Sunday school continued. Among other things, it pointed out the insanitary conditions and the distress caused to the children by the smell and noise of the neighbouring slaughterhouse.

Towards the end of the 19th century government became more directly involved with education. A law making education compulsory for children under 10 years was passed in 1876, but the historic milestone occurred in 1891 with the introduction of free education. Finally, in 1902, an Education Act was passed abolishing the old School Boards which had been set up in 1870. On 1 July 1903, two years after the death of Queen Victoria, the four National Schools in Leatherhead were taken over by the Surrey County Council and the age of state education began.

## Other schools

St John's School came to Leatherhead in 1872 from St John's Wood, London, where it was founded in 1851. The headmaster here was the Rev. E.C. Hawkins. At the start there were about sixty-five pupils, but the school expanded considerably during the next 30 years and by the turn of the century there were nearly 300 boys attending. The Rev. A.F. Rutty was Headmaster from 1883 to 1909 and much of St John's progress was due to him.

About the same time that St John's moved to Leatherhead, another boarding school for boys was opened at the corner of Grange Road and Leatherhead Road. This was for boys from 8 to 13 years old and was later to become Downsend School, but at this time it was known simply as the Leatherhead Road Boarding School. The Headmaster was the Rev. A.T. Scudamore and the school accommodated 14 boys. By 1890 the school had the name of Gateforth House Preparatory School and five

years later it became Downsend School with 25 boarders and 25 day boys.

There were a number of other private schools which came and went and have left no records, but the one at The Mansion lasted into the 1870s. It was known as The Mansion Grammar School for Boys and was started about 1846 by Dr. Thomas Payne. He taught the advanced Jacotot system of education based on the principle that because all men have equal God-given intelligence they have the ability to instruct themselves in everything. This Jacotot method implied an educational freedom which many Victorians found shocking. The school was a boarding and day school for about fifty boys from 10 years upwards. Dr. Payne was succeeded by one of his assistant teachers, Robert Ibbs, in 1866. Leatherhead also had a Mechanics' Institute which was in North Street and for a moderate fee it ran courses on all kinds of practical subjects. Evening classes from chemistry and carpentry to dressmaking and shorthand were also held in the Institute and sometimes in one of the local schools.

## Literary and artistic associations

Edward Lear, the artist and writer of humorous verse and limericks, was associated with Leatherhead through his sister Eleanor, who lived most of her married life in Church Street and died there. She was married to William Newsom, a director of the Bank of England. Eleanor Newsom wrote regularly to her brother when he was travelling abroad and in 1874, when in India, Lear wrote home to say that the cool of the Ootacamund Hills reminded him of Leatherhead.

Robert Louis Stevenson knew the area well and many are the stories of George Meredith's strenuous walks over the Mickleham and Leatherhead Downs from Box Hill, where he lived and wrote for over 40 years. Swinburne, Hardy and Sir James Barrie used to visit him there. Thackeray and Conan Doyle both wrote about the area. The Rev. John Honeyman is a Leatherhead curate in

Thackeray's *The Newcomes*; and in Conan Doyle's *The Speckled Band* the action takes place near Leatherhead. Sherlock Holmes and Dr. Watson take a train from London to Leatherhead, hire a trap at the station inn and drive for a few miles through the Surrey lanes. The novelist Anthony Hope was the son of the Rev. E.C. Hawkins, Headmaster of St John's School. He wrote *The Prisoner of Zenda* in 1894 and *Rupert of Hentzau* two years later. He died in 1933 and is buried in the churchyard.

Pre-Raphaelite painter William Holman Hunt, famed for his *Light of the World*, found romance in Leatherhead. Through the sculptor Thomas Woolner, he met and married Fanny, one of the eight beautiful daughters of Dr. George Waugh. Hunt and his wife went to the Middle East where she died, leaving him with

**77**   Emily Moore at 82 years of age.

a child. He later married her younger sister Edith.

Another painter, Edward Wilkins Waite, was born here in 1854, son of the town's Congregational minister and one of eight children. Three of his brothers became artists and two were musicians. Edward Waite conducted the Abinger choir which won at the Leith Hill Festival in 1905. He was educated at The Mansion Grammar School in Leatherhead. After two years in Canada, he returned to take up painting seriously. He died at Fittleworth, Sussex in 1924. Public interest in his paintings, described as poems of the English countryside, has recently revived.

Other less familiar painters who were living in the town at this period included Henry Grey, a landscape artist, Henry Hall Knight and William Snow. Unlike them, Cecil Aldin was known for his sporting paintings. In his mid-teens, while a student at the Royal College of Art, he was commissioned by Emily Moore, the proprietor of the *Swan Hotel*, to paint her terrier. He stayed in the town for about six months, getting commissions from local people to paint their pets. Later he exhibited at the Royal Academy and lived until 1935.

There were also musicians: the Middleton brothers, Alfred and James, lodged with their families in Highlands Road and were professors of music, while a third brother was the owner of travelling marionettes.

Other residents included Matthew Moggeridge, journalist and editor of *Social Notes*, and George Ryder, the naturalist.

## A look at the parish

The parish church continued to play an important role in the town's affairs and Leatherhead was fortunate in having a trio of vicars so devoted to the welfare of their growing community at this time.

Benjamin Chapman came of a distinguished Yorkshire family. He was appointed to Leatherhead in 1836 and actively sponsored the first National School for Boys and later other

schools. The Vicarage was brimming with children for he had three sons and seven daughters. He had spent part of his early life in Sweden and had written biographies of Gustavus Adolphus and Gustavus Vasa, and at Cambridge he won the Porteous Gold Medal for the best theological essay. He made some improvements to the church, started a fund to renovate the organ and established the choir in its modern form. He died in 1871 and the church's altar reredos was erected in his memory.

Thomas Thompson Griffith was vicar of Leatherhead for only five years (1871-6) but in that time he built a new vicarage (which is still standing) and supported a major restoration of the church. Graduating from Clare College, he was Precentor of Rochester Cathedral for 11 years. Griffith left Leatherhead in 1876 to become Rector of Seale.

Frank Ernest Utterton, who exchanged livings with the previous rector, was only 31 years old when he came to Leatherhead in 1876, but later in life he grew a long white beard and children thought 'he looked like Moses'. He had never less than two or three curates to

**78-80**   Three Leatherhead vicars. *Above left*, Benjamin Chapman, *above right*, Thomas Griffiths and *below* Frank Utterton.

assist him plus a licensed reader. He arranged for yet another church restoration and was the force behind the building of All Saints' church and school. With his wife, he gave parties at the Vicarage for the choir, the Mother's Union, the Sunday schools and other schools, the Girls' Friendly Society, the Temperance Society and other good causes. He encouraged the provision of soup kitchens to help the poor during the winter months and opened the Rose Coffee Room as a social centre. The Parish Room in the Fairfield was controlled by him. He founded the *Parish Magazine* in 1880 which is still published today.

Utterton loved travel, describing in the *Parish Magazine* his visits to the Holy Places. He was obviously a physically active and fit man for in 1894 he was awarded the Royal Humane Society's medal for rescuing a boy in Yorkshire's River Wharfe. He was a Canon of Winchester and was later Archdeacon of Surrey. One of the first members of the newly formed Urban District Council, he died in 1907 and the stained glass east window in the church is dedicated to his memory.

## Sports

The Leatherhead Cricket Club was founded in 1850. By the 1880s Leatherhead played on average 32 matches in the season. Every August there was a cricket week, Leatherhead playing the MCC in 1892 and the next year a team grandly called 'The World'. They drew with the MCC but easily beat 'The World'. The cricket grounds were a recreation area next to Kingston Road and a field in St John's School.

The town's football club was founded about 1887, taking its name Leatherhead Rose from the Rose Coffee Rooms in Kingston Road which became its headquarters. The club ground was in the Kingston Road area, but for some years in the 1890s it played at Thorncroft Manor.

Leatherhead Athletic Sports Association was founded in 1888. It held its annual meet-

ings on Easter Monday in the St John's School grounds. A Girls' Tennis Club was formed in 1895 with courts at Thorncroft Manor. In 1901 the Institute had at least one tennis court. The swimming baths were built in 1888 in one of the large barns of the mill on the River Mole. Local boys, many of whom had no bath at home, often took soap and towels with them and swam in the small bathing hole near Randalls Park. The Surrey Union Hunt met at the *Bull* in 1852 and on Leatherhead Downs in October 1857. Late in the century, the kennels of the Mid-Surrey Draghounds were at Downside in Leatherhead. Other sports included polo, played at Hawks Hill in Fetcham by many from Leatherhead's hunting fraternity, and a form of amateur horse-racing on Epsom Downs in winter, the races being known as the Leatherhead St Leger and the Leatherhead Derby. There was fishing in the Mole, rich in trout, and golf was played on the Downs near Cherkley Court and privately at Polesden Lacey.

## Pastimes and celebrations

There were many inns: the *Swan*, *Duke's Head*, *King's Head*, the *Bull*, the *Running Horse* in Bridge Street and, in Kingston Road, the *Plough*, *Royal Oak* and the *Railway Arms*. On Saturday nights the town was full of late-night shoppers listening to the town band playing outside the *Duke's Head* in the High Street or in front of the clock tower in North Street. There had been a Town Band since 1881, and though decimated by the First World War, after which it was disbanded, the Silver Band has recently been revived and renamed in 1974 the Mole Valley Silver Band.

In Victorian Leatherhead there were plenty of street musicians, buskers and other itinerant showmen, hurdy-gurdy men always with monkeys, performing bears, and Italian organ-grinders. There was even a mini 'Speakers' Corner' at the square below the town clock where 'anarchy and atheism' was preached from a soap box. On May Day, young men and girls fixed nosegays of spring flowers on poles and

**81 & 82** The *Duke's Head*, *c.*1850 and *c.*1900.

danced round them throughout the day. In early June the town would be full of excited racing people going to and coming from the Epsom races, especially on Derby Day. In the autumn, usually on 11 October, there was a town fair. Only a few weeks later there were the jollifications of Guy Fawkes Night, with fireworks and bonfires. On New Year's Eve the townspeople danced to the Town Band in the street and sang 'Auld Lang Syne' by gaslight under the town clock at midnight.

In summer the Horticultural Show was usually held in marquees in the gardens of one of the large houses. The Town Band usually played and the day again ended with dancing. Leatherhead was prone to celebrate at the slightest provocation; for instance, there was much memorable boating at a Water Carnival

**83** May day outside the *Old Bull* in 1905.

**84**   Emily Moore with a friend, possibly Ellen Terry.

in July 1901. The Town Band played on the island in the centre of the river while circled by a stately procession of illuminated boats.

The cinema was too new to be more than a curiosity, yet a cinematograph show was given at the Institute in October 1898 and another at the Victoria Hall early in the following year. At a lecture on recording in October 1897 given by the Edison Bell Company, Canon Utterton made a short speech into a machine which repeated it 'with startling accuracy'.

Many entertainments were held in the Institute hall and on one occasion the music hall star Albert Chevalier appeared. In quieter moments, draughts, whist and bagatelle were played here, and there was a circulating library which still operates today. Penny Readings, a modest concert form with songs, music and recitations, were often held for charity. In April 1893 the Royal Nubian Minstrels, the ancestors

of the Black and White Minstrels, performed and the Royal Handbell Ringers entertained. Victoria Hall, later to become the Leatherhead Theatre in the High Street, was another place of entertainment. But the Assembly Rooms at the *Swan Hotel* were the most prestigious meeting place in the town. Emily Moore, the proprietress, was famed for her sumptuous table, providing food for the yearly horse sales at Hampton Court attended by the Prince of Wales (later King Edward VII). Many sought references from her before employing servants as a guarantee of their sobriety. She was a close friend of singer Jenny Lind and actress Ellen Terry. Royalty came to Leatherhead on three occasions in the 1880s and 1890s, and each time it was the HRH The Duchess of Albany, who twice came over from Claremont to present the prizes at St John's School; the third time she opened a fête at Thorncroft Manor which lasted for three days.

**85**   The *Swan* yard.

**86**   The *Swan*, *c*.1865, which was a regular stage-coach stop where horses were changed and refreshments supplied to the passengers. Although it may seem a romantic way to travel, it was risky and uncomfortable with frequent breakdowns, highway hold-ups and coach sickness brought on by poor suspension and appalling roads.

**87**    Bridge Street is decked in flags and bunting for Queen Victoria's Diamond Jubilee celebrations.

But celebrations at these fêtes were as nothing compared to the way the town threw itself into the Jubilees in June 1887 and 1897. On 21 June 1887 the streets were decorated with bunting, loyal banners and portraits of the Queen. At 7a.m. the church bells rang a celebratory peal and there was a huge procession to the church for a morning Thanksgiving Service after which there was lunch for 269 people at the *Swan*. This was followed by a children's treat at Randalls Park where about 775 sat down to tea and cakes, each going home with a Jubilee mug. After dark, large crowds thronged Highlands Road on their way to its highest point near the reservoir. There, after the Leith Hill rocket gave the signal,

Leatherhead's rockets were fired and a huge bonfire was lit. The 1897 celebrations were similarly jolly and so impressive that the local paper likened the town to Venice at carnival time.

The mood was soon to become sober with the outbreak of the South African Boer War at the end of the century. With Lawrence Potts as chairman of the LUDC, Leatherhead made its contribution to comforts for the troops and put its music into concerts for disabled soldiers and their families. Then, early in 1901, Queen Victoria died. There were black borders round the *Parish Magazine* and muffled church bells to mark her passing after a reign which lasted over 60 years.

*Chapter Seven*

# The Twentieth Century

### Edwardian times and the prelude to war (1901-14)

In the first year of Edward VII's reign Leatherhead continued to send comforts to the troops still fighting in the Boer War. When this ended in May 1902 the town's celebrations were quickly followed by preparations to mark Edward VII's coronation. This was intended for 26 June but the King had appendicitis and it was postponed until 8 August.

Leatherhead decided a fitting memorial to the late Queen Victoria would be a new hospital, the Cottage Hospital in Clinton Road having closed in April 1902, £130 in debt. Walter Cunliffe of Tyrrells Wood gave the land in Epsom Road and the foundation stone for the Queen Victoria Memorial Hospital (later Victoria House) was laid by Mrs. Alfred Tate of Downside in October 1903. The hospital was opened two years later and served the sick

**88**  The Queen Victoria Memorial Hospital in 1909. It later became Victoria House.

**89**   The School for the Blind building was completed in 1904.

of Leatherhead for nearly forty years. The School for the Blind completed their building in 1904. Accommodation was provided for 250 pupils and with 15 acres of ground there was room for expansion. Reputed to be the finest school of its kind in Europe, with King George V as its patron it became the Royal School for the Blind.

New house building in the 1900s was mainly in the Fairfield, Kingston Road and Highlands Road areas. Queen Anne's Gardens, off Linden Road, was built in 1903 and in the next few years the lower part of Copthorne Road was developed for housing with Woodville Road, Kingston Avenue, Clinton Road, Reigate Road and St Nicholas Hill. All the new houses had electricity, which the Town Council in 1902 had at last agreed to. The Leatherhead and District Electricity Company was formed and their works established beside the River Mole.

This spurt in housing was mainly due to the increase in the town's population. Between 1901 and 1911 this grew from 4,694 to 5,491, at double the rate of the previous decade. This may have led to an over-full labour market, since in 1903 there were 100 unemployed, perhaps 10 per cent of the total working population. Leatherhead and District Commercial Association was formed in 1908 to improve trading, which was not helped by a serious fire in Mould's High Street store early that year. It began late at night in the large warehouse next to the shop and quickly enveloped both. There was a huge explosion caused by gunpowder and cartridges, stored on the top floor, igniting. The Leatherhead, Epsom and Dorking fire brigades spent most of an exceptionally cold night trying to put out the flames. Water from the hoses froze as sheet ice on the High Street, making it difficult for the horses drawing the fire engines to reach the site.

More headlines were made when a four-year-old boy George Dench fell from Thorncroft Bridge and was saved from drowning by postman Harry Dancer, who was later decorated with the Royal Humane Society medal. George Dench himself joined the church choir in 1914 and was still a member until his death in August 2001. His brother Sidney was chosen as one of the firing party at the Cenotaph for the inauguration of the tomb of the Unknown Warrior.

ALFRED G. VANDERBILT.

**90**  Alfred Vanderbilt aboard his personal stage-coach *The Venture*.

The poor, disabled and aged welcomed the imaginative Lloyd George-inspired Insurance Act of 1911 which protected them through illness or unemployment by creating the doctor's panel and the insurance stamp. It supplemented rather than eliminated the work of the Friendly Societies. With pensions for the old granted in 1908 and the introduction of the weekly half-holiday in the Shops Act of 1911, this proved to be a period of great social benefit and a small first step towards the welfare state of the 1940s.

The first bus service between Leatherhead and Guildford began as the First World War started, with other bus services to Clapham via Epsom and Ealing via Kingston. The railways with their inexpensive excursions were increasingly popular yet a few well-to-do still travelled by private stage-coach. The *Venture*, owned by the American millionaire Alfred Vanderbilt, often called at the *Swan* on its way from London to Brighton driven by Vanderbilt himself. He lost his life when the *Lusitania* was torpedoed in May 1915. Three years earlier, there was another marine tragedy when the *Titanic* went down on her maiden voyage and Harvey Collyer from Leatherhead was drowned but his wife and young daughter were rescued.

On 24 February 1913 Mrs. Emmeline Pankhurst was held in the new police station in Kingston Road. Accused of conspiring to place gunpowder in Walton Heath Golf Club tea pavilion, frequented by Lloyd George, she was committed to the Surrey Assizes after a night in Leatherhead, where it is said the Chief of Police gave up his bedroom for her. Her case was dismissed.

Mrs. Pankhurst was not the first suffragette to brave Leatherhead. Four years before, in 1909, a meeting of the Women's Freedom League (suffragettes) had been held in the square before the *Old Bull Inn*. Two of the suffragettes, Mrs. Despard and Mrs. Grieg, were on a proselytising tour of the southern counties travelling in a horse-drawn van with 'Votes for Women' on its chassis. The mostly male crowd

**91**   *The Venture* reaching the *Burford Bridge Hotel* on its way to Brighton with guests.

of between 400 and 500 was so noisy when the open-air meeting began that the ladies could not be heard above catcalls and the ringing of a loud handbell. They moved the meeting to the relative safety of Victoria Hall where entrance was for ticket holders only. Even so, the mob scaled the roof and the whole activity bordered on a riot with the police outnumbered, so the meeting was cancelled.

On the outskirts of the town, another game of high politics was being played by Sir Max Aitken, later Lord Beaverbrook, who lived and died in 1964 at Cherkley Court, his main country home. This ebullient, ambitious Canadian, the M.P. for Ashton-under-Lyne in 1910, dominated the newspaper world in the first half of this century. Cherkley was an ideal

place for politicians to meet, manoeuvre and plot. Herbert Asquith, Prime Minister for the first part of the First World War, Bonar Law, F.E. Smith (Lord Birkenhead) and Lloyd George were frequently there. In spite of his friendship with Asquith, Beaverbrook succeeded in bringing down his government and replacing him with Lloyd George. For this he was given a peerage and became Minister of Information and later Minister of Munitions in 1918. In 1918 he launched the *Sunday Express,* the *Evening Standard* and a number of Scottish newspapers. He continued in politics and through his newspapers he advocated Empire Free Trade and in the 1960s campaigned against Britain's entry into the Common Market.

**92**   Cherkley Court in 1910 was built by Abraham Dixon and later became the main country home of Sir Max Aitken, Lord Beaverbrook.

## Leatherhead in the First World War (1914-18)

In response to Lord Kitchener's appeal, many of the town's young men joined up. Indeed, most of St John's school leavers went straight into the forces. (Their school had been completely gutted by fire in 1913 but by 1914 had been rebuilt.) An Emergency Relief Committee was set up; the postal services had declared in early August that the Leatherhead signal station would maintain day and night telegraphic communication with Dover. The reservoir was guarded by Boy Scouts by day and the Church Lads' Brigade by night. By September the town council rightly thought boys aged 9-11 were far too young for such an onerous task and the Water Company took over the responsibility.

At the end of September 1914, several hundred soldiers of the Universities and Public Schools battalion (UPS) of the Royal Fusiliers arrived to be billeted locally. King George V inspected them on Epsom Downs on 17 October and later Lord Kitchener and the French War Minister did the same. Those stationed in Leatherhead left shortly afterwards for Epsom and thence to France, promising to write to their hosts; tragically few survived the battle of Delville Wood to do that.

The town was also receiving wounded Belgian soldiers, 30 of them coming on 28 October to The Red House which had been converted into a Red Cross hospital and convalescent home, still run by its owner, Mrs. Burton. More wounded were expected and a Belgian Refugee Aid Committee, chaired by the Rev. E.A. Downes, Headmaster of St John's School, was set up. Three houses were made available for the duration of the war and by March 1915 over 25 Belgian refugees were living there.

During 1915, two Leatherhead men received posthumous awards for bravery: an old Johnian, 2nd Lieut. J.H. Woolley of the Queen Victoria's Rifles (TA), was awarded the Victoria Cross in April, the first Territorial in the war to receive it; the Albert Gold Medal was awarded to 2nd Lieut. Grey de Lisle Leach of the Scots Guards who died on 3 September 1915 from wounds received in a grenade accident in France while saving the lives of his own men. He was the son of C.F. Leach of Vale Lodge, who was very much a major benefactor of the town once described as 'one big family with Mr Leach as father'. He gave the land for both the war memorial and the new Leatherhead Hospital in 1940, which he endowed. A ward was named after him and another after Dr. Von Bergen, a much-loved local physician.

By midsummer 1915 there were said to be over 400 Leatherhead men serving in the forces, and a plea for medical supplies and sand-bags to be made by those at home brought a response and workrooms were opened. Mrs. Leach forwarded new-laid eggs weekly to London hospitals for wounded soldiers and by

**93**   The fire which completely gutted St John's School in 1913.

the end of the year over 4,680 eggs had been dispatched. Miss Brown of Church Terrace was enterprising enough to take family photographs to be sent to the forces overseas.

In the middle years of the war, soldiers were said to be 'marching through Leatherhead with guns all day' and aircraft flew over the town daily. Indeed, one came so low that the pilot was able to ask the way to Brooklands! Later that year, Lieut. Maurice Le Blanc Smith, a Royal Flying Corps pilot, paid an unorthodox surprise visit to his parents and landed, damaging his plane, on the Forty-Foot Road recreation ground.

Little joy came with the first white Christmas of the century in 1916. Fear of enemy air attacks led to the official banning of external lights after dark and fines were imposed for non-observance. Dr. Marie Stopes, then living at Craigvara in Belmont Road with C. Aylmer Maude, was one of those prosecuted.

Leatherhead's high casualty rate led to an early call for the fallen to be commemorated, and on 21 March 1917 the Bishop of Winchester dedicated a war shrine on the wall of the clock tower in North Street. The shrine was a triptych of fumed oak carved by C.E. Grantham from a design submitted by the donors, the women of Leatherhead. This was later moved to the parish church and the present memorial unveiled in 1921.

The last spring of the war was black, with the Allies severely pressed and no real hint of peace to come. In War Weapons Week in June, the Lord Lieutenant, Lord Ashcombe appealed for funds for the forces. Other simple comforts like letters from home were somewhat restricted since after 75 years the penny post for letters was raised to a penny halfpenny.

Nevertheless, a few months later the war was miraculously over and on Armistice Night there was a huge bonfire outside the *Old Bull* hotel. The final mattress to burn managed to set fire to three large elm trees and yet the crowd happily sang, cheered and danced for peace had returned to their lives.

## Between the wars

With the death of the last town crier, Joseph Longhurst, in 1923, the town slowly began to change. Large estates were broken up and in the mid-thirties the *Swan Hotel*, the centre of the town for 300 years, was demolished and redeveloped. The swan over its porch was subsequently discovered in a Fetcham garden in 1990 and restored by Sheila Warner. It now nests in the museum garden.

In all 983 Leatherhead men had served in the war and 163 gave their lives. On 19 July 1919, the day chosen for the nation's peace celebration, 350 returning servicemen were given a grand lunch at St John's School. Afterwards a procession of 2,000, led by the vicar of Leatherhead and the council chairman, made their way to Randalls Park. There were sports and tea for all and dancing until dusk when the Silver Band led the way to Yarm Court for the lighting of a bonfire and fireworks, the time-honoured way for the town to celebrate. In this case the euphoria was short-lived, as the reality of hard post-war years came with the twenties.

## The Twenties

The Leatherhead Urban District Council was much concerned with the high cost of living, which had risen one-and-a-half times since 1914. It believed the way to alleviate some of the hardship was to provide and manage cheap rented houses for those on low incomes. So the first council houses were built early in 1921 in Poplar Road. In all 59 houses were built and preference was given to ex-servicemen and their families. It was another four years before the second group of 90 council houses were built, this time in Kingston Road. There was of course plenty of private house building as many of the large estates were broken up. Elm Bank, opposite Thorncroft Manor, was sold in 1924, and developed into the St Mary's Road housing estate. Likewise, Tyrrells Wood was also put on the market. The Golf Club took it over in 1924.

**94** The Roll of Honour originally on the wall of the clock tower was donated by the women of Leatherhead in 1917 and moved to the parish church in 1921.

**95 & 96**   After the demolition of the *Swan Hotel* in 1936 the swan over its porch disappeared but was found in 1990 in a Fetcham garden. The swan was restored and placed in the garden of Hampton Cottage, Leatherhead's museum.

**97** Peace celebrations were held in July 1919 with the Silver Band to the fore.

Another large house and grounds to come under the hammer was Givons Grove. Its owners, H.V. Roe, the aircraft manufacturer, and his wife, the sex educationalist and birth control pioneer Dr. Marie Stopes, moved to Hindhead. Dr. Marie claimed she needed 'intelligent youth, Leatherhead being too grown up for her'. She later returned to live at Norbury Park. In another part of the town, in Ermyn Way, the Long House was sold to the Ex-Service Welfare Society for the Mentally Disabled and renamed Frederick Milner House. It is now a nursing home.

In 1923 the town's first Roman Catholic church was built in gothic revival style in Garlands Road. It was donated by Sir Edward Hulton who lived at Downside. He joined his father's newspaper business in Manchester in 1885 and produced the *Daily Sketch* in 1909. He was knighted in 1921, sold his four publications for £36 million, and retired in 1923 with a reputation for producing commercially successful publications quite free from political interference. His son, also Edward, was raised in Leatherhead and succeeded his father, becoming chairman of Hulton Press. With the

**98 & 99** The Royal Mail stamps of 1992 used the stained glass window designs by Paul Woodruffe from Our Lady and St Peter's R.C. Church, Garlands Road.

closing in 1957 of his most brilliant experiment in photo-journalism *Picture Post*, he too was knighted. The church boasts stations of the cross designed by Eric Gill and stained glass windows used in 1992 as designs for Royal Mail Christmas stamps.

The break-up of the large houses and their estates was taking place when living conditions were at a low ebb for many because of the country-wide industrial troubles which culminated in the 1926 General Strike. Leatherhead

found 300 volunteers to drive lorries, trains and other vehicles. The strike began to crumble in just over a week. It was in the year of the General Strike that Leatherhead opened its first purpose-built fire station in River Lane to house its first motorised fire engine. The previous machine had been housed in the clock tower in North Street and was drawn by horses stabled in Bridge Street. It was arranged that the Gas Company call the Fire Brigade by sounding a hooter when the fire alarm bell rang in the post office.

**100**   Frederick Milner House, once the Long House, was sold to the ex-Service Welfare Society.

**101**   Leatherhead's first motorised fire engine was named after the Lord Mayor of London's daughter and featured in the Lord Mayor's Show.

## After the General Strike

By 1931 there were 6,916 people living in the town. New industries set up, like the Rayon Manufacturing Company in Ermyn Way employing 300 and the Cable Manufacturing Company in the Kingston Road. On a smaller scale, Lady Zoe Hart-Dyke began silkworm farming at her home, The Wilderness, at the entrance to Tyrrells Wood in 1932. She and her husband first bought 5,000 silkworm eggs which hatched, and silk threads from the cocoons were spun on a large hand-reeler in their garage. Eventually more space was needed and a small out-factory was opened near The Warren, Epsom Road. This had to close mainly due to an injunction taken out by a neighbour, Lady Duckham, who complained that silk-making produced a very unpleasant smell. Eventually work was transferred and thrived in Sir Oliver's ancestral home at Lullingstone Castle. The silk made by the Hart-Dykes has been traditionally used for royal coronation and christening robes ever since.

## Farming

Farming itself had changed over the years. The in-filling of Bradmere Pond at the foot of Bull Hill in 1905 was perhaps a hint of changing times, although a horse trough to replace it had been thoughtfully presented by Mrs. Braybrook. Horse ploughing continued up to the Second World War, and until 1925 there was still a pound for stray animals near the *Plough* in Barnett Wood Lane with a fine of one shilling to claim an animal back.

The once labour-intensive harvesting was certainly revolutionised by the rapid reaping, threshing and baling of the combine harvesters

**102**    The Bradmere Pond at the foot of Bull Hill was filled in in 1905.

and by the general use of tractors. As a result, the need for only one or two men to carry out in hours what had previously taken several days, inevitably reduced the numbers of agricultural labourers.

Leatherhead continued mixed farming with a balance between cereals and livestock. Some old farms like Prewetts in Cleeve Road were ultimately taken over by Unigate but others, like Bocketts Farm and Highlands Farm, carried on independently. Early in the century, Highlands Farm began harvesting mint and lavender and the town was filled with its scent as it was carted to Mitcham for the making of mints and lavender water.

The Mizen Brothers, Surrey market gardeners, had extensive land by the mill pond in Fetcham in 1921. There were eight acres of watercress beds and 15 acres of glasshouses where asters and ornamental ferns were cultivated on the largest scale in England at that time. In wartime salads and tomatoes were grown, but after the Second World War the business slowly declined and ceased trading in 1957. The Leatherhead Bus Garage, now replaced by offices, and the Water Board took over part of the land. It was near the site of the present fire station in Cobham Road, Fetcham that in 1929, during the digging of celery beds, finely worked Saxon objects of bronze were unearthed.

**Services**

The Leatherhead and District Water Company was replaced by the East Surrey Water Company in 1927 and the water was softened. In the period up to 1939 the new water managers built the present pumping station, with its four large bore-holes deep in the chalk, and the Elmer softening plant on Hawks Hill. Today, with even more sophisticated equipment, Leatherhead's water continues to be maintained to a high bacteriological and chemical standard; no fluoride has been added.

The Southern Railway, formed in 1923, began an electrification programme. In July

**103** The nameplate of the last of the Schools class locomotives, No. 939, was *St John's* and is displayed in the school's entrance hall.

1925 the Waterloo to Effingham Junction line as well as the Waterloo to Dorking line, both via Leatherhead, were electrified while steam trains continued to run to Dorking and beyond until the mid-1960s. There were at least three steam engines named *Leatherhead*: LBSC 5a 1872-80, LBSC 178, 1890-1912 and SR 939, 1935-61. No. 939 *Leatherhead* was the last of the 40 'Schools' class locomotives named after leading public schools; it was 'St John's, Leatherhead'. One of the original nameplates from the engine is on permanent display in the entrance to St John's School.

With the Southern Railway operating, the LSWR station was no longer needed and was closed down on 10 July 1927 leaving the one station where it is today. Railway excursions to London and the south coast resorts intensified to compete with cheap charabanc tours. For shorter journeys there were at least half a dozen bus services operated by the East Surrey Traction Company, with pick-up points in the High Street at the *Swan Hotel* and the *Bull Hotel*.

With all this development there was a growing awareness of open spaces and in 1929 this prompted Frank Benger to found the Leatherhead & District Countryside Protection Society. The formation of Leatherhead's Chamber of Commerce in 1929 superseded the Commercial Association founded 21 years before. Ironically, the financial collapse on Wall Street heralded another period of world depression which affected the town seriously just when its fortunes should have flourished.

**104**    Turning point of one of the early motorised buses, at the *New Bull.*

## The Thirties

The unemployment rate in Leatherhead was probably higher than it had ever been since the First World War. In order to alleviate this, the LUDC set up a special committee in January 1933 which proposed that everyone should pay a shilling a week towards the cost of public works to be put in hand. This unemployment support scheme gave rise to jobs such as making a car park on Bull Hill and resurfacing St Nicholas Hill. Money was also set aside to supplement the state unemployment payment. The council declared that no married man should have less than £2 a week to live on. This is a fair indication of how low the standard of living was for Leatherhead's poorer residents. Even so, in 1934 Surrey adopted Jarrow, an even more distressed area in the north.

Low trade turnover in the town led to many shop closures. Some stayed empty for many years. Granthams, the furniture-makers, was still operating although in May 1933 its head, Charles E. Grantham, died. A trustee of the Institute, he was also the founder in 1906 of the Leatherhead Operatic Society. Its first performance was *The Pirates of Penzance* in Victoria Hall in 1907. Its most memorable was probably an open-air production of *Merrie England* in Randalls Park in 1922 and again in 1937. 'Queen Elizabeth I' arrived by river on the state barge and in 1922 her progress was limited by a real thunderstorm in the first act.

The town's spirit was indomitable even in hard times and in January 1932 the Leatherhead Rotary Club was formed to lend a charitable hand. In March 1934 the British Legion set up a relief committee in Leatherhead to assist needy ex-servicemen, while the disabled were heartened by the Cripples' Training College acquiring Leatherhead Court School building in Randalls Road. It was opened in November 1935 by the then Duchess of York, now Queen Elizabeth the Queen Mother. The College took her name in 1942, becoming Queen Elizabeth's Training College for the Disabled. The founders were Dame Georgiana

**105** Dorincourt was originally Leatherhead Court School until 1934, when it became the Queen Elizabeth Training College for the Disabled.

**106**  The changing crossroads. The top of Bridge Street in 1912 still has Wilde's teashop and bakery on the right, but below, in 1928, the bakery is replaced by a mock-Tudor building.

Buller and Stanley Evans, an orthopaedic surgeon. The Queen Elizabeth's Foundation includes the training college and Dorincourt estates. These consist of Banstead Place, an assessment centre for handicapped teenagers, and a mobility centre, Dorincourt itself, with work-shops, residential hostel and arts centre, and Lulworth Court, a holiday home at Westcliff.

A year after his Silver Jubilee in 1935 King George V died and Leatherhead dedi-cated the memorial gardens on Bull Hill to him. A tree was planted to mark George VI's Coronation and a colourful procession through the streets took place while the church bells rang a coronation peal. As Duke and Duchess of York, the King and Queen had spent their honeymoon at Polesden Lacey, the home of the Hon. Mrs. Greville who later became Princess Margaret's godmother.

Throughout the 1930s Leatherhead was changing dramatically in appearance. Despite pleas from the Countryside Protection Society, many buildings were torn down regardless of their age. Kingston House, bought by the council in 1930, was demolished three years later and what is now called Wesley House was built in its stead.

In spite of being described as 'a gem of Georgian architecture', the Manor House, near the present Thorndike site, was demolished. It was the home of Herbert K. Reeves, truly a town benefactor, who moved to The Mansion in 1923. He sold that to Surrey County Council in 1950 and donated 21 acres of his land in Fetcham Grove to the council who, with further land from Major Howard, eventually built the Leisure Centre on the site. Mr. Reeves, who died in 1959, gave Sweech House and

**107**   In 1923 Herbert Reeves, the town benefactor, moved to The Mansion on the left in Church Street.

**108**  Randalls Park House, the last house of that name on the site, was owned by the Henderson family. The grounds were purchased by Wimbledon Borough Council for use as a cemetery and in 1951 a crematorium was added.

other buildings on Gravel Hill to the Countryside Protection Society and Sweech House was fully restored in 1950. Land and money for the church hall in Church Road was donated by him and the hall's Reeves Room commemorates his generosity.

Even more indefensible than the destruction of the Manor House was that of the *Swan Hotel* which closed in September 1936 and was sold for development. The council had been equally indifferent to the pulling down of the old *King's Head Inn* in 1929 and had not demurred when Emlyn House together with the *Old Bull* hotel were demolished. However, Surrey County Council did acquire Norbury Estate on Fetcham Downs. In 1932 LUDC protested at Wimbledon Borough Council's purchase of Randalls Park grounds from John Henderson for use as a cemetery and took their case unsuccessfully to the House of Lords. In

1951 the cemetery came under the Borough of Merton and in 1961 a crematorium was added. The chapel was mindlessly destroyed by arsonists in 1986 and rebuilt in 1987.

In 1936 the Leatherhead Gas Company was taken over by the Wandsworth Gas Company, who provided high pressure mains gas so that by April 1938 gas-making ceased in the town. The industry was nationalised and North Sea gas was connected in 1971. The Gas Company's offices were on Bull Hill. In North Street, the Congregational church had been sold in 1934 to the Guildford and District Industrial Cooperative Society. By 1930 the old building next door to the slaughterhouse had become very dilapidated, and rats ran over the back pews during evening service, so it was decided to build a new church, Christ Church in Epsom Road, now the United Reformed church.

**109**   The *King's Head* in the High Street, 1920. It was demolished in 1929.

**110**   North Street and Bull Hill. Only just visible on the left is the gas offices. The council offices are directly ahead with the famous cedar in front which was felled in 1966.

One of the council's principal worries in the thirties was the same as in the twenties—traffic congestion. This became worse as the years passed and in June 1933 the London *Evening Standard* claimed that, at weekends, Church Street had 'one of the worst bottle-necks round London'. Automatic traffic lights had been installed at Swan Corner, since on Sundays 850 cars an hour passed through. The traffic was eased appreciably by the completion of the Leatherhead by-pass.

Few realised early in 1939 that by the autumn the country would be at war. Yet as early as October 1937 air-raid precautions started with an appeal for 800 volunteers to act as ARP wardens. By February 1938 these wardens visited most homes to demonstrate how to wear the government-issue gas masks. Both the Red Cross and the Women's Voluntary Service (WVS) joined the Civil Defence, and it was not surprising that the town's arrangements were said to be the best in Surrey. The Chief Warden was J. O'Hea, founder of the Colt Group which later, in 1968, was the centre of the 'I'm backing Britain' campaign.

### The Second World War (1939-45)

When war broke out in September 1939, a small National Defence Committee was set up in the town which purchased and requisitioned cars and lorries and designated the bus garage as a temporary decontamination centre and mortuary. It was some months before anyone was put to the test, Leatherhead's first concern being to welcome and house the child evacuees from Streatham and Dulwich. Troops from the Royal Corps of Signals were later billeted in the town. Ration books were issued to all and there was also a Fuel Office for controlling the amount of coal and petrol used.

Leatherhead suffered losses early in October 1939. Four local men died (two of whom were cousins) when HMS *Royal Oak* was torpedoed in the comparative safety of Scapa Flow. There followed seven months of the so-called 'Phoney War' when there was little activity during the winter and spring of 1939/40. Nevertheless, a state of readiness was maintained by frequent exercises. With three or four appliances, some firemen later joined the nightly convoys to London to help beat the fires of the Blitz.

Churchill, who had in his lean years often written for Beaverbrook, appointed him Minister of Aircraft Production in May 1940 and Lord Privy Seal in 1943. It was in the former role that he made an indispensible contribution to victory in the Second World War. His appeal for light metal and aluminium pans and saucepans for aircraft manufacture was a nonsense yet, as a journalist, he knew that, in contributing them, people felt they were helping to win the war. In 1942 Cherkley itself was bombed and set on fire and then Lord Beaverbrook moved to Wellbottom Cottage in his grounds. This later became the home of his doctor Alan Everett, who had practised in Leatherhead for over 50 years.

There were concerts and films at the new Crescent Cinema to keep the spirits high. In August 1940 another cinema (St George's, formerly the Picture House) opened in Victoria Hall. There were dances at the *New Bull Hotel* and the composer Dr. Ralph Vaughan Williams gave talks, the last being at a concert with the Surrey String Players conducted by Kathleen Riddick.

The realities of war returned to the town in June with the arrival of 78 sick and wounded men from the British Expeditionary Force. They were taken to the Blind School Hospital, having had a 'miraculous deliverance from the Germans at Dunkirk'. Many more casualties were cared for in Leatherhead's new Cottage Hospital in Poplar Road. Opened in May 1940, it replaced the Queen Victoria Memorial Hospital in Epsom Road, now Victoria House. Charles Leach, advised by Dr. Von Bergen, acquired the present site from Windfield estate and donated it to the town. Whether by foresight or good fortune or both, building materials were

**111**   The Cottage Hospital, Poplar Road, was opened in 1940.

delivered by 1939 and so escaped the wartime clampdown on new buildings.

Both the hospitals were soon needed when, during late 1940 and early 1941, Leatherhead suffered many enemy bomb attacks. The first was on 27 August 1940 when 20 high explosive bombs were dropped near Ashtead Common. Several houses were damaged but there was miraculously only one casualty. Three days later about 60 high explosive bombs fell in a line from Yarm Court to Crampshaw Lane, Ashtead in a daylight raid in which five people were killed. In September, the month of the Battle of Britain, there were three raids. The Leatherhead Golf Clubhouse received a direct hit, two cyclists luckily survived bombs exploding only 30 yards from them, and on

30 August a land mine fell in a garden in Gaywood Road, Ashtead, killing four and injuring others.

People were now being evacuated from London in large numbers and in September 1,000 arrived to be billeted in Leatherhead. October was just as bad as September for bomb alerts, nine falling in a line from Southey Hall, Great Bookham to the Leatherhead by-pass, damaging shops, offices and houses. Two bombs fell on oil storage tanks at the waterworks and burning oil crept through the drains to the River Mole, taking nearly 24 hours to put out. Early in 1941 the first incendiary bombs were dropped, possibly jettisoned by retreating German planes being chased away from London. Hundreds fell between Hawks Hill and Ashtead, lighting up the surrounding hills; Fetcham Downs was likened one night to a huge candlelit Christmas tree.

After that, there was a long period from 1942 to the end of 1943 when no bombs fell on the town and the government ordered a cut in ARP staff. At its peak period there had been almost 800 ARP personnel, mostly part-time volunteers, in the town. By now public air-raid shelters had been completed capable of holding 1,012 people. Previously the caves under the Swan Brewery site, once used as a store for beer barrels, had provided shelter from the air raids. Surrey's first British Restaurant was opened in 1941 and soon it was serving 300 meals a day. There was a Nelson flag day, a concert at the Crescent Cinema with songs by Isobel Baillie, Anne Ziegler and Webster Booth, and a sketch *Nelson at Leatherhead* written by Frank Benger. The destroyer HMS *Scout* was adopted by the town and a plaque commemorating this, once displayed on the ship, was hung inside Wesley House.

Canadian forces had been stationed in the town since 1940 and a new road, Young Street, bridging the River Mole, was built by them on the outskirts of the town. Named after the Canadian commanding officer, Major Young, it was to by-pass the town's streets which were too narrow for tanks and other armoured vehicles brought for repair. The Canadian Air Force units were stationed at Tyrrells Wood while others were at The Mansion, Vale Lodge and Thorncroft Manor where, to commemorate their stay, they planted two maples, their national tree, close to the north side of the house.

Early in 1942 the RAF moved into Victoria House in Epsom Road and made it a recruiting office. Once more a grand Savings Fair was held, this time in St John's School in July, when a Whitley bomber gun turret lent by Archibald Frazer-Nash was on display. Captain Frazer-Nash was a remarkable man whose contribution to the war effort was immense. His gun turrets were produced by Nash and Thompson, a subsidiary of Parnell

Aircraft during the war. Made at Tolworth, Surrey, Swindon and Bristol, they were fitted to many British bombers as well as to some armoured vehicles, flying boats and torpedo boats. One turret, from a Vickers Wellington bomber ditched in Loch Ness, was rescued to be lovingly restored and, with another, is displayed at Brooklands Museum. The year ended with world-famous pianists Pouishinoff and Mark Hambourg performing at the Crescent Cinema, while in November the church bells rang out to mark a turning point in the war, the victory of El Alamein.

The gallant defence of Stalingrad by their Russian allies caught local people's imagination. Late in 1943 the King presented Stalingrad, now victorious, with a gold and silver sword fashioned by RAF Corporal Leslie Durbin whose wife, artist Phyllis Ginger, was the grand-daughter of the gardener at the *Swan Hotel*.

In the summer of 1944 the quasi-peacetime for Leatherhead sadly ended with the dropping of V1s, flying bombs known as 'doodle-bugs'. These were pilotless high-explosive craft launched from the French coast which landed indiscriminately when their fuel expired. Sixteen fell on the area, the most serious at Chaffers Mead and Thorncroft Manor. Two hundred houses and 32 shops were badly damaged and the church clock stopped. The last bomb in the district, a V2 supersonic rocket, fell close to City of London Freemen's School in February 1945. The windows of 50 houses were broken but there was only one casualty.

In all, 591 high explosive bombs and over 4,000 incendiaries fell on the Leatherhead area. Nearly 3,000 houses had been damaged and there had been 800 air-raid alerts. There were 112 casualties, 11 fatal (including three ARP workers). After the war, the ARP services commemorated their dead comrades by presenting the LUDC with a coat of arms which includes the first and only symbol of civil defence in heraldry, a portcullis chain surrounding the fire.

## From War to Peace (1945–50)

Peace came and many of the restrictions were lifted; the nightly black-out ended and there was light in the streets. No longer was the wail of the air-raid sirens (operated in working hours by the staff of Barclays Bank) heard and VE-Day 'Victory in Europe' in May 1945 was celebrated as Leatherhead always celebrated: there was a victory parade through beflagged streets, a bonfire at Swan Corner and open-air dancing. The church was floodlit and this time its bells rang a victory peal as a thanksgiving service was held in Elm Bank Gardens. All the joy was repeated on VJ-Day 'Victory in Japan' in September, the focal point being the clock tower; a huge bonfire was lit at the top of Bull Hill for roasting a pig and there was dancing and singing and parties for the children. Sadly, six children out of the 41 evacuees still living in the area could not go home because their homes had been bombed and some because their parents could not be traced.

By 1946 most of the troops had left the area. Leatherhead's fighting men were slowly coming home. Some took part in the great Victory Parade in London when 40 trainees from Queen Elizabeth's Training College had a privileged view from seats in the forecourt of Buckingham Palace.

In the same year the new Prime Minister Clement Attlee and his wife came to Leatherhead to ceremoniously release the Stepping Stones over the Mole at Box Hill from being 'out of bounds', as they had been in the war. And in the peace of the churchyard the grave of a German airman W. Mennig Mann, shot down over Leatherhead in 1940 (and later re-interred in Germany), was faithfully tended by the parents of Pilot Officer Edward Arnold whose own grave lay nearby.

## The modern town

In 1946 the Leatherhead and District Local History Society was formed with A.W.G. Lowther as its first chairman. One of its aims was to produce a history of Leatherhead and

**112**   The town's Coat of Arms, which included a flame encircled by a portcullis chain, the symbol of civil defence. The river and its valley is symbolised by blue and silver waves with green wedges while the swan rising above the wreath refers to the river and the *Swan Inn*. The stag's head and book in the lower part of the shield refer to the City of London Freemen's School and its association with other schools in the town.

this was achieved in 1988. Over the years the Society has published further histories of the surrounding villages as well as many reports on the research of its members. Many of these are on sale at Hampton Cottage, now the town's museum in Church Street. Once the home of a falconer in 1682, Hampton Cottage is a timber-framed building which was acquired and restored by the Society in 1976. Always interested in preserving, sometimes with the Countryside Protection Society, what is left of

**113**   The clock tower that originally housed the fire engine became a public lavatory and was demolished in 1952.

Leatherhead's old buildings, it has recently, with a sponsor, helped Mole Valley District Council erect plaques on some of them giving brief histories.

In 1951, although the war was now six years away, the rationing of food and clothing still continued. Few were yet able to enjoy foreign travel because of strict currency regulations. However, better times seemed to be on their way as London staged the Festival of Britain on the South Bank of the Thames and Leatherhead mirrored this with its own Festival

that summer. But, with the winter, there was a time of mourning ahead. First there was the loss of two landmarks: the great three-ton cedar tree outside Wesley House in 1966, and the clock tower. Originally built to house the town's fire engine in 1859 at a cost of £129 4s. 2d., the tower had the clock added in 1860. Latterly, it became a public lavatory and was demolished in 1952.

In February 1952 the church bells muffled their peals on the day of King George's VI's funeral. His daughter Princess Elizabeth was

Queen. With its long history of celebrations, Leatherhead excelled itself on 2 June 1953, the Queen's Coronation Day. There was a parade followed by five hours of entertainment given by no fewer than 22 local organisations at the football ground. The following day, Sunday, there was yet another procession, 2,000 strong, to attend an open-air Service of Thanksgiving at Fetcham Grove. The Operatic Society staged another appropriate production of *Merrie England* (this time inside the Crescent Cinema) with professional singers Anne Ziegler and Webster Booth in the lead. So the new reign began and so did a new way of life when food rationing, the last of the wartime restrictions, was removed nearly 10 years after the Second World War ended.

## Leatherhead's schools

Leatherhead's schools were now overcrowded and the problem was not resolved until 1953 when the juniors from All Saints' moved into the Kingston Road school, which became Leatherhead County Primary junior school, and All Saints' reverted to being an infants' school. At the same time part of the senior school, known by then as the Leatherhead County Secondary, moved into new premises in Dilston Road, but it was to be more than 20 years before the whole school was united under the same roof. In 1964 the school was named Therfield when the Headmaster, Mr. Claytor, discovered that it stood on land presented by King John in 1205 to Brian de Therfield.

In 1935 there was a Roman Catholic school in Leatherhead started by five nuns from the Order of St Andrew. Opened at 'Hillfield' off Grange Road, the school nearly came to an untimely end in March 1941 when a land mine fell on the building but no one was killed. The senior school was eventually rehoused in 'The Knoll' in Epsom Road and the junior school in Grange Road. In 1952 the foundations for a new senior school were laid on the hockey pitch site at 'Hillfield' and the whole building was completed in four months. Eventually

St Andrew's became a co-educational comprehensive school in 1971.

The period between the two world wars was a time of considerable modernisation and expansion for both St John's School and Downsend. After the Second World War, Field Marshal Viscount Montgomery became chairman of St John's School council until 1966. 'Monty', himself a parson's son, always took a keen interest in the school which had been founded for sons of clergymen. A new chapel was dedicated in 1963 and further specialist blocks were built. Downsend was acquired in 1918 by A.H. Linford with only one pupil. Numbers quickly built up and in 1921 Mr. Linford was joined by his son; together they ran the school until the Second World War when A.H. Linford retired. Christopher Linford joined his father in 1966 and remained as principal when his father retired in 1977. So the school has been run by three generations of Linfords for over 80 years.

One of the more celebrated girls' boarding schools was Leatherhead Court School founded by Miss Martha Wood-Tullis in 1904 and closed in 1934. One of her ex-pupils, Winifred O'Shaughnessy de Wolfe Hudnut, married Rudolph Valentino and another was Eleanor Roosevelt. The Misses Mary and Blanche Hewlins ran three private schools in Leatherhead over a period of 33 years. Oxford House School at 4 Lower Terrace, Bridge Street for boys and girls from five to seven and girls up to the age of 11 closed in 1907. The Miss Hewlins moved to The Crescent where they set up a school for young ladies which lasted for about three years. In 1915 they moved back to Bridge Street where they established the Dudley House School for boys and girls from five to seven which was always known as 'Miss Hewlins' School'.

The Lindens, like Downsend, opened with only one pupil in 1918 as a kindergarten and preparatory school in Linden Pit Path. In 1935 it moved to Park Rise and Miss Josephine Ingram, its founder, retired to be succeeded by Miss Frances Marsden, who was in charge for

**114**   The original Downsend House acquired by A.H. Linford in 1918.

44 years. By 1965 there were over 200 pupils, and on Miss Marsden's retirement in 1971 the school was taken over by Downsend School and renamed Downsend Lodge. The Rowans in Epsom Road, opened in 1949, also started with only one pupil but within four years there were 137. In 1960 it was taken over by Clarks College. In September 1987 it also became another Downsend Lodge.

A School of Music opened in 1926 and a Secretarial School in Bridge Street. Both are now closed.

## The Royal School for the Blind

By the mid-thirties the school had become a place of residential workshops rather than an educational establishment. With the Second World War, it was requisitioned by King's College Hospital. It was not until the 1950s, when the Chelsea Pensioners housed there finally left, that it was once more a School for the Blind. Twenty years later the whole emphasis had shifted from that of an institution segregated from the local community to a place where residents are encouraged to be independent and join in the life of the town. The provision of flats has enabled some of the residents to marry, the first wedding taking place in 1982. The building has recently been sold and Reeves Court, built in its grounds, houses a resource and activities centre. The school has been renamed Seeability with headquarters in Epsom.

## Some of the town's industries

Ronsons, founded in America in 1898, originally made church ornaments. In 1918 it began manufacturing cigarette lighters and the rights to sell and service the lighters in the UK were acquired. In the Second World War Ronsons moved to Leatherhead from London and bought Dorincourt where their war work was making, among other things, bomb fuses. These were manufactured on government-subsidised machinery which after the war was modified to make lighters. Five million lighters were produced before Dorincourt was sold in 1953 to Queen Elizabeth's Training College and Ronsons moved to its custom-built factory in Randalls Road. Here the firm developed butane and battery lighters. However, the Japanese, Ronsons best customers, produced their own lighters, not only inexpensive to buy but incorporating a competitive piezo mechanism. The US parent corporation had long been in difficulties yet desperate attempts by Ronson UK to solve the corporation's financial problems only resulted in the liquidation of Ronson UK and the sale and subsequent demolition of the Leatherhead factory in 1981.

At the east end of the town was Goblin BVC, makers of vacuum cleaners, washing machines and clocks who employed 1,000 workers. The founder was Hubert Cecil Booth. In 1904 he produced the world's first portable vacuum cleaner which only needed two

**115 & 116** Hubert Booth who designed the world's first vacuum cleaner and moved his factory from Fulham to Ermyn Way where he established the Goblin Works. The cleaner was bright red, had a 5 h.p. piston engine and needed a team to operate it. It was patented in 1901.

operators, one to pump the bellows and the other to operate the cleaning tool. In 1921 his company produced the first electric upright bag model and later the cylindrical model. In 1938 Goblin BVC moved to a complex in Ermyn Way and during the Second World War made munitions which included mine-sinkers, shell fuses and camouflage netting. Post-war, Hoover became a major competitor and so dominated the market that vacuum cleaning became known as 'hoovering'. Nevertheless, Goblin had diversified and itself contributed to the generic vocabulary with Goblin 'Teasmade'. H.C. Booth died in 1955 and Goblin, in spite of expanding in 1959 to manufacture miniature electric motors (some used in Concorde), slowly had to run down its organisation. It finally closed in 1984 and the valuable site on which it stood

was eventually taken over by Esso, who made it their headquarters in 1990.

Also based in Leatherhead is ERA technology, an independent, self-supporting research and development organisation. With a staff of scientists and engineers, ERA's activities extend from the design of microwave antennae for satellite communications to the investigation of solid-state devices in power engineering, and include such diverse topics as the fundamental aspects of dielectric materials, plasma etching, engineering metallurgy and the application of microprocessors for automation and control. PIRA, the Printing Industry Research Association, is also in Randalls Road as is the British Food Manufacturing Industries Research Association. Many software companies have moved into the Mole business parks as office

**117** Logica is among many businesses that have established themselves in the town. Its graceful building by the refurbished railway station is one of many in 30 countries providing a global solution to the integration of IT systems.

**118** The Edward and Eleanor sundial in Tunsgate, Guildford. Executed by Richard Quinnell, it was designed by Ann Garland who used to live in Vale Lodge.

**119** An early photograph of Rowhurst Farm, a mid-16th-century building adjacent to the forge and Fire and Iron Gallery belonging to the Quinnell family.

blocks are rapidly replacing houses and shops all over the town.

Far away from high technology is the wrought iron forge and works of Richard Quinnell in the Oxshott road, founded in 1937. Richard Quinnell himself has been a prime mover in the revival of the blacksmith's art. His work and that of fellow metalsmiths are on display in his Fire and Iron Gallery, which is part of the land adjacent to *Rowhurst*, a 16th-century timber-framed building said once to have been a hunting lodge of Hampton Court Palace. Still in the arts, Surrey Sound, a professional recording studio established in 1975 in Kingston Road, has been used regularly by top musicians and groups such as Paul McCartney, Cliff Richard, the Police and Godley and Creme.

**120 & 121** Malcolm and Donald Campbell and Priors Ford, once the home of Donald (now called Campbell Court). In 1966 he parked his proposed *Bluebird*, on the right, next to *Bluebird* 7 and his own 'E' type Jaguar. He was killed on Coniston Water in 1967 when his craft disintegrated while achieving a speed of over 300 m.p.h. Both he and the vessel have recently been exhumed. The wheel of an earlier *Bluebird* was given to the town museum by his daughter.

## The Thorndike Theatre

In 1966 the Crescent Cinema in Church Street was pulled down and the Thorndike Theatre built upon the site. As the 'Leatherhead Repertory Theatre', it was originally housed in the old Victoria Hall which, in spite of having a tiny stage, pigeons in its corrugated roof and rats in the basement, was taken over by the Under Thirty Group of young professional actors in 1950. With Jordan Lawrence as artistic director, it succeeded where two previous companies failed.

As its audiences grew larger, there was an obvious need to rehouse the company. Dame Sybil Thorndike gave her name to a new theatre to be built on the site of the Crescent Cinema. Managed by Hazel Vincent Wallace, it was designed by Roderick Ham. The Thorndike won him many awards including one for its amenities for the disabled. The theatre was opened in 1969 by Princess Margaret. The company itself was glad to move, not least because of the tragedy in the old theatre when the Green Room manager was murdered in 1968 by a deranged young man later found unfit to plead.

122 The Thorndike Theatre contract is signed by chairman Greville Poke watched by Michael Marriott and Dame Sybil Thorndike (seated), Hazel Vincent Wallace and Joan MacAlpine in 1968.

123 Dame Sybil in her dressing room when she last appeared at the Thorndike to celebrate her 90th birthday in a recital with John Casson and Leon Goossens.

Over the years, the Thorndike became a real arts centre with exhibitions, films and concerts, and a studio theatre in the Casson Room developed by Joan MacAlpine. With inevitable budget problems, however, the theatre, now a listed building, closed in 1997 in spite of attempts by Bill Kenwright and Sir Peter Hall among others to save it.

It has recently been taken over by an evangelical group, Pioneer People, who have plans to renovate and refurbish the theatre, retaining its stage.

## The changing town

In 1976, at a meeting convened by the Leatherhead Society, there was public support for the restoration of the community facilities of the Institute, in particular for the restoration of the main hall which had been out of use for over 30 years. With professional advice and many volunteers from the Leatherhead Community Association and others, the work was completed and the hall opened on 18 July 1987. Named the Abraham Dixon Hall after the Institute's founder, the ceremony was made a family occasion with two of his descendants, Michael and James Dixon, being present. The Institute is now the base for a library and many affiliated clubs, which happily is how the founder envisaged it in 1893.

The LUDC replaced the swimming pool at West Wing with a Leisure Centre opened in 1975 complete with many sports facilities and a water park.

## The Swan Centre

Preparations for the building of the Swan Centre began in 1979 with the demolition of the *Prince of Wales* public house in Lower Fairfield Road and some of the houses in Middle Road which lay in the path of the future Leret Way. In conjunction with this, a one-way traffic system was introduced round Station Road, Randalls Road and Bull Hill in March 1981. It was then possible to close the High Street to through traffic. Church Street was also closed as far as The Crescent and full and controversial pedestrianisation of the inner town was introduced.

The official opening of the Swan Centre was on 4 November 1982, and for the first time Leatherhead shoppers had a partially covered arcade with an integral car park. This backs on to the one-way system and has the effect of shielding, some say fortifying, the town from the prying eyes of visitors. The whole

**124** The *Prince of Wales* public house was demolished to make way for the Swan Centre.

**125**    A car destroyed on the Epsom Road by a tree during the Great Storm of 1987.

development, the most drastic transformation since the town was laid out in the 12th century, epitomises the neo-traditional architecture of the 1980s. The very names appeal to the past: Leret Way (after the Domesday form of Leatherhead) and Swan Centre (after the inn regrettably demolished in the 1930s). When the Swan Centre was completed the M25 motorway was well advanced and the route from Wisley to Reigate and on, through Leatherhead (junction 9), was opened on 6 October 1985.

After the overflowing of the River Mole in 1968, when Fetcham was virtually cut off and the bridge closed, it was difficult to visualise it reduced to a trickle as it was in the drought of 1976. That was the hottest summer of this century, only rivalled by the summer of 1826 in the previous century. Temperatures were high for months and the year ended equally memorably with a white Christmas.

Another record in extremes was reached in the winter of 1963 when the mean temperature all over England was -30° with nine consecutive days below freezing in the month of January. The Thames above Kingston froze

so that it was possible to walk across the river. There is no doubt that the great storm that swept through southern England in the small hours of 16 October 1987 was not as severe as the Great Storm of 1703 which blew off Leatherhead's church spire. That storm killed over 8,000 people, while in 1987 there were, thankfully, relatively few casualties. Nevertheless there were 15 million trees lost locally, thousands of blocked roads, disrupted telephone, gas and electricity services and damaged buildings.

The sound of traffic was silenced by impassable roads and replaced with the shriek of chainsaws as essential highways and driveways were cleared. Local names like Givons Grove, Beech Avenue and Tyrrells Wood overnight lost some of their significance while the mammoth task of repairing the damage, inspecting trees and clearing wrecked woodland took many months—in some cases, years.

And so it is with the townscape of Leatherhead, like a woodland felled and replanted, and as yet not comfortable with every new format designed to revitalise what was once a town at the crossroads.

# Index

Page numbers in **bold** refer to illustrations